HUMAN DESIGN UNLOCKED

Discover your energy type and harness your power

ALEXANDRA FULLERTON

PAVILION

Pavilion
An imprint of HarperCollins*Publishers* Ltd
1 London Bridge Street
London SE1 9GF

www.harpercollins.co.uk

HarperCollins*Publishers*
Macken House
39/40 Mayor Street Upper,
Dublin 1
D01 C9W8
Ireland

10 9 8 7 6 5 4 3 2 1

First published in Great Britain by Pavilion
An imprint of HarperCollins*Publishers*
2025

Copyright © Pavilion 2025
Text © Alexandra Fullerton 2025

Alexandra Fullerton asserts the moral right to be identified as the author of this work. A catalogue record of this book is available from the British Library.

ISBN 9780008705848

This book contains FSC™ certified paper and other controlled sources to ensure responsible forest management.

For more information visit:
www.harpercollins.co.uk/green

Publishing Director: Laura Russell
Commissioning Editor: Lucy Smith
Editor: Shamar Gunning
Copyeditor: Lisa Pendreigh
Editorial Assistant: Daisy Gudmunsen
Junior Designer: Lily Wilson
Senior Production Controller: Grace O'Byrne
Proofreader: Kate Reeves-Brown
Indexer: Lisa Footitt

Image on page 2 courtesy of Shutterstock

Printed and Bound in the UK using 100% renewable energy at CPI Group (UK) Ltd

All rights reserved. No part of this publication may be reproduced, stored in a retrieval system, or transmitted, in any form or by any means, electronic, mechanical, photocopying, recording or otherwise, without the prior written permission of the publishers.

Without limiting the author's and publisher's exclusive rights, any unauthorised use of this publication to train generative artificial intelligence (AI) technologies is expressly prohibited. HarperCollins also exercise their rights under Article 4(3) of the Digital Single Market Directive 2019/790 and expressly reserve this publication from the text and data mining exception.

The reader is reminded that Human Design is a spiritual and metaphysical practice. The information in this book is not intended to replace or conflict with professional medical advice. Always seek the advice of your GP or other qualified health providers with any questions you may have regarding a medical condition. Any use of information in this book is at the reader's discretion and risk. This publisher and the author disclaim liability for any medical and/or legal outcomes that may occur as a result of applying the methods described by the author in this book.

For Jerry Ophelia Fullerton

My Manifesting Generator 6/2 - you are destined for magic (although anyone who orbits you will know that anyway) xxx

CONTENTS

1	**What is Human Design?**	1
2	**How Human Design can improve your life**	13
3	**How to use this book**	31
4	**Types**	42
	Generator	46
	Manifesting generator	54
	Manifestor	62
	Projector	70
	Reflector	78
5	**Strategy**	86
6	**Authority**	99
7	**Centres**	134
8	**Profiles**	161
9	**Next-level learning**	187
10	**Beyond this book**	213
	Further reading	226
	Acknowledgements	229
	Index	231

WHAT IS HUMAN DESIGN?

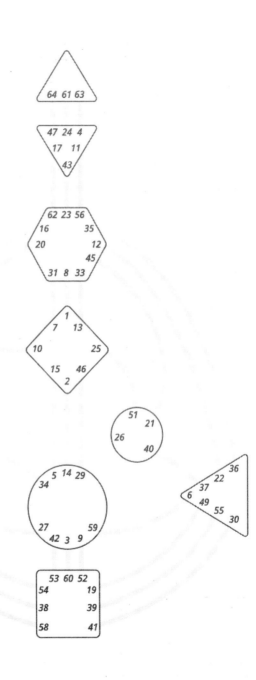

WHAT IS HUMAN DESIGN?

Chances are you are looking for something. Most of us are. You might have read up on each religion or faith and experimented with every esoteric practice out there. Or perhaps you have landed here straight off the bat. Either way, you probably want to understand your place in the world, you are searching for guidance and answers to *all* the big questions. Maybe you just need a handbook for adulting.

Human Design can help with all the above conundrums of modern life *and* set you up for a brilliant future. Human Design is neither a religion nor a cult, it is a perfect blend of the metaphysical and scientific, which is based on genetics. You do not need to believe in an afterlife, worship a god, follow a guru or carry out a set of rituals or actions. With Human Design, the answers are there within you, irrefutably set from before your birth. Your path, your interactions, your purpose are already set. All that is needed is for you to lean into the learnings and allow yourself to align with the energies within you (this comes from your Inner Authority, see page 37), then you will be well on your way to becoming the absolute best, most authentic version of yourself (when you are living in your Signature, see page 37). Every one of the 8 billion people on the planet has the resources within them to flourish under Human Design's principles (although granted, their circumstances are wildly different and in many cases deep conditioning and environment may prohibit their involvement with the system).

Human Design goes deep, looking at the myriad ways our energy centre influences how we exert energy and how we are affected by those around us. It gives you a toolkit for dealing with those occasions in which you will thrive (your Type, see page 37), the best way to respond (your Strategy, see page 37), as well as advice on how to remove yourself from those situations in which you are not going to operate at your optimum (your Not-Self Theme, see page 37). While the positions of the planets at the time of your birth are key, going beyond astrology and your sun sign, Human Design also takes into consideration the Hindu Brahmin chakra system, the teachings of The Tree of Life from Kabbalah, the divination method of the I Ching, biochemistry *and* genetics, all wrapped up with the satisfaction of the Myers-Briggs personality assessment.

Compared to many other esoteric practices, Human Design is the baby of the bunch. While crystal therapies, Reiki and astrology have been around for thousands of years, Human Design only came into existence in the 1980s. However, it calls on many historical metaphysical practices and combines them with the science of genetics to create the ultimate method for understanding the best way of being you. Perhaps that is why it is not as widely known as the other methodologies... yet. In Summer 2024, #humandesign had 454 million views (and rising) on TikTok. Human Design is a truly New Age theology, perfectly placed to chime with our planets' switch from the Age of Pisces into the Age of Aquarius.

What is the Age of Aquarius?

Astrologers believe that the earth moves through momentous ages, which define society and our collective experience. Each age lasts around 2,150 years (the approximate time that it takes the vernal – or Spring – equinox to shift from one constellation into the next, reflecting what is visible in the sky just before dawn) and we are moving out of the Age of Pisces into the Age of Aquarius. Unlike the astrological procession of sun signs, the great ages travel through the signs in reverse, so after Aquarius we will move into Capricorn, then Sagittarius.

Some suggest that we are already in the Aquarian age, although many believe it will begin around the year 2600. Although astrologers cannot agree on an exact start date, it is widely accepted that we are living through an age of transition, during which time the old ways cling on for supremacy while new systems emerge. It is a wild ride punctuated by fanaticism, unrest and conflict. While the Piscean Age has been defined by rigid religion and strict hierarchies within government and state, the Aquarian Age is more aligned with technology, innovation, personal awareness and equality. The Age of Aquarius is not all peace, love and flowers in our hair, but the themes of the era will allow for some epic changes... and for the better, if we embrace it.

THE ORIGINS OF HUMAN DESIGN

So, if now is the most opportune time for Human Design to reach a wider audience, when did it begin? Rewind to 9 April 1948 when Alan Krakower was born in Canda and went on to grow up within a well-to-do family. He worked in media and enjoyed creating music before he upped sticks, leaving his home to travel and landed in Ibiza. It was on the White Isle where Krakower had a mystical experience. While in deep mediation over a period of eight days and nights, a voice of superior intelligence transmitted all the knowledge and information about the workings of Human Design to Krakower, along with asking him, 'Are you ready to work?'

Sceptics might look away now and roll their eyes, but there are elements of more than mere coincidence that follow this origin story. Krakower changed his name to Ra Uru Hu and spent the reminder of his life teaching Human Design around the world until he passed away in 2011. Unlike other gurus, Ra took his role in the story of Human Design as that of founder and messenger and yet he did not request belief in him or encourage disciples. Ra simply taught Human Design as the most perfect information system for living and was often quoted as saying, 'Do not believe me.'

And those coincidences? While Ra was receiving transmissions from the Voice, a supernova was visible to the naked eye over Chile and was showering our planet with three times more neutrinos than normally make it to earth. Neutrinos are ultra-light, subatomic radiation particles that can pass through matter. Every single second, more than a trillion neutrinos from the sun pass through your body at almost light speed. The Voice told Ra that the neutrinos raining onto earth were how life force energy would travel through every being in the universe. While scientists had discovered neutrinos in 1956, they were described as dark matter and, as they are so tiny, they are hard to detect. Ra was told that neutrinos carried mass, so were able to pick up and pass on information wherever they go, rather than being empty vessels. Now, here is the thing: it was not confirmed that neutrinos could carry mass until 1998 (remember, Ra was told they *could* in 1987). A key element of Human Design is the understanding that at the moment we are born, the matter and cosmic information from the planets around you is deposited in your being, your very genes, and that cosmic energy (passed on via neutrinos) will determine your entire life ahead. There are other elements within Human Design that seem more than purely coincidental, which we will return to later.

Alongside the genetic code that makes you *you*, every human is surrounded by an electromagnetic energy field (your aura) on which Human Design places huge importance. The different centres in your body, which are defined or undefined, will angle the energy of your aura and affect how you receive the energy of others. There are four aura types. When you meet someone in person, you might be highly attuned to understanding their aura, you may describe a like or dislike in terms of their vibe. In Human Design, how you take in and give out energy is key, and it is all down to your unique aura.

WHAT IS HUMAN DESIGN?

As our belief systems move towards an ever-secular society, away from the rigid structures of organized religion that dominated the Age of Pisces, perhaps there are still vestiges of belief running through us that fortune telling, metaphysical practices and New Age beliefs are wrong. Thoughts of the occult can still stir up fear. But while Tarot cards, for example, are linked heavily to mysticism, Human Design, though thought of as a mystic New Age practice, is actually robustly pragmatic. Human Design is not a methodolgy based on superstition or sorcery. Simply put, when you know your habits and your energy givers (or energy takers), you can take steps to live in a manner that will be most productive for you.

To define your Type and your Aura, Human Design does use several more mystical methods to reach this insight. From Western Astrology, Human Design takes your specific time of birth to determine your conscious gifts along with noting where the planets were 88 days before your birth (when your consciousness was formed) to work out what your unconscious gifts are. The 360-degree astrological wheel informs the archetypes of the zodiac, which are then broken up into smaller archetypes using the I Ching.

What is the I Ching?

The I Ching is a divination method based on the writings in an ancient text, which originated from China's Zhou dynasty over 3,000 years ago. Users ask a question and 64 hexagrams give suggestions to the question's possible outcomes, via answers outlined in an accompanying book (cited as one of the first books ever written). If you are keen to experiment, questions can be based on any element of your life, such as asking whether you should trust a certain person or the next steps to take in your work, as well as general advice on how to find peace in a situation of conflict.

When we explore your Body Graph, which is the key to decoding your individual Human Design, you will notice there are 64 gates and – remember those coincidences – 64 corresponding codons in the structure of human DNA. These parallels are one of the reasons Human Design is often described as a science and has more acceptance than traditional New Age beliefs. The science to back up the system is clear.

Human Design also relates to the Hindu Brahmin chakra system and includes seven chakras in each of our bodies, plus two additional energy centres unique to Human Design: these denote our aura energy centres. The teachings of the Zohar and Kabbalah religion's Tree of Life inform the Human Design belief that pathways allow energy to flow through your Centres and Gates (again, more on these later, see page 38).

As a philosophy shared by a white man from the Global North, including prominent elements from Indian, Chinese and Jewish cultures, it is important to consider whether Human Design is cultural appropriation. There is a significant element of whitewashing across the entire wellness sphere, which is vital to address. Just think of every spa with a statue of Buddha at its entrance. This book cannot answer whether Human Design does culturally appropriate, as your own moral code will guide you, but if you are benefitting from any methodologies or theories that originate from other, less dominant cultures than your own, respect for the entire people is essential. As is education. I advise that you do your own research on each of the methodologies mentioned to truly understand their place in Human Design, and therefore your own life.

Human Design's acolytes often describe the system as a science as they study their own behaviour, while Ra Uru Hu shared further ideas for the development of each of the traditional methodologies, along with further thoughts on genetics, to create its whole. Compared to very obvious cultural appropriation in the fashion world, for example, when a white designer takes Mexican motifs and repackages them to sell for great profits but does not credit or compensate the original creators, potential cultural appropriation in Human Design is a far more complex issue. Cultural appreciation, rather than appropriation, is a more considered space in which to live and open conversation should always be welcomed alongside the experiences of Human Design that lie ahead of you.

HOW HUMAN DESIGN CAN IMPROVE YOUR LIFE

HOW HUMAN DESIGN CAN IMPROVE YOUR LIFE

Right now, you are likely to be shaking your head in disbelief at the state of the world, the country and your very own life. Doesn't it feel *hard*? From politics at home to climate change and humanitarian crises across the globe, the world is in a mess. What is more, everything is now magnified through the lens of social media and the judgement of strangers as to how you are handling it all. Add in the pressure to excel at your career (while building a lucrative side hustle); having a wide circle of witty friends; being the best daughter/son/sister/brother/parent/guardian you can be; staying out of debt; replying to all your incoming WhatsApp messages immediately *and* drinking enough water… Exhausted yet? You are not the first to realize that adulting is hard. Many have lamented the lack of a guide to navigating grown-up life, but Human Design can help. Who would not want the chance to improve their life and understand its purpose? Human Design offers methodologies, techniques and ideas – all completely tailored to you – that will show you the best way to become your most authentic self, which in turn will lead to a smoother, easier, happier life ahead.

IDENTIFY CONDITIONING

Part of the problem stems from the world in which we live. Unless you have been holed up on the dark side of the moon, you cannot help but be influenced by a set of attitudes and expectations that we have all been conditioned to abide by and strive for. Society has set us up to yearn for material possessions, status and success, following rigid strategies to smash those goals. Those that do not conform are frowned upon at best, or ostracized at worst. Even the ideal for beauty is conditioned. Not everything in the world that conditions us is bad, however, as many laws and codes in society keep us safe and healthy. More often than not, the rules, fears and beliefs about how we can and *should* be accepted, successful, fulfilled and loved can be limiting.

Let's take the norm of working nine to five. Only when we were plunged into a global pandemic did businesses consider that there might be another, equally productive way to work. It felt revolutionary that employees could fulfil their roles without travelling to a workplace, to sit physically alongside their colleagues for a set timeframe, and in some cases be more productive. But what if you have never been the type of person who thrives on working in that way? Perhaps you do your best thinking at 6am or, conversely, you are most productive from midnight into the wee small hours. Understanding your Human Design will show you the best working patterns for your Type. It is then up to you to work towards living with those patterns... *and* noticing the difference in your being.

As humans we are all teetering between the need to be unique as an individual and craving to belong and be part of a tribe. Perhaps this harks back to our days living in caves, when living away from a group was *not* the safest option, but in modern society this need to be among your peers no longer serves the same purpose. Living in such proximity can actually be damaging as we constantly search for acceptance. Comparison culture – a form of 'keeping up with the Jones' – is not a helpful way to exist, but so much of our current conditioning encourages it.

In Japan there is a proverb, 'the nail that stands out must be hammered down.' Ouch. But if you know that you are meant to stand out, that you have different talents, a unique purpose, an individual operating mode *and* a practical strategy for living, through discovering your Human Design, you can take the first step towards breaking out of the cycle of conditioning and developing true self-awareness. Human Design will help you use your gifts in the most authentic, smoothest way that aligns with your energies. When you are living in a high-vibe, energetic state, you will be aligned to the universe. The universe absolutely wants you to be successful in the way that suits your uniqueness.

Human Design gives you insights for understanding exactly how you should approach relationships (both romantically and with friends and family), how to tackle decision-making and the best ways for you to be in the workplace. It also provides a checklist for finding environments in which you will thrive, the best foods for you to eat, and even when you are primed to take in nourishment *and* knowledge.

Pretty much everyone on earth will have wondered at some point (some more often than others), why am I here? Why are any of us here? What am I doing with my life? What's my purpose? Your beliefs and conditioning about your path and future may not line up to your true purpose, which is why adulting feels so damn tough right now, but once you have discovered where your talents lie and how to use them to the highest alignment, life will begin to feel so much easier.

KEEP A DECONDITIONING DIARY

It's all very well telling you that deconditioning will be key to your Human Design journey, but I also wanted to share some practical advice to help you achieve this. This section offers key actions to guide you and solid steps to take. Deconditioning will make more sense as you learn about your individual Type, Strategy, Centres and Authority (which we will explore shortly…) but I've included these steps near the start of *Human Design Unlocked*, so that as you make progress on your own journey, you can look back on how far you've come!

If you have ever had coaching or undergone therapy you'll be familiar with the concept that you have power over your thought processes. When you need to break out of negative or harmful thinking, or bring about a change in any part of your life, deconditioning follows the same methods. Whether through coaching, 'unlearning' or Cognitive Behavioural Therapy (CBT), personal development notes your current behaviours, questions them, works out *why* you're taking that action then consciously changes that process for a more beneficial one.

Many times you'll act, think or speak because it's what you *should* do. Sometimes it's because you've taken on other people's energies as your own. Once you are aware of this and have acknowledged that it's not true to you, it's time to replace that action (whether it's thoughts or physical processes) with something more authentic to your own self and your Human Design.

Free from expectations, you can create space for happier, healthier habits. As with many elements of Human Design, there is science behind the cosmic magic. Our brains physically develop grooves as our thoughts, words and deeds follow established neural pathways. Whenever we break those patterns and do (or think or say) something new, we develop new neural pathways. Stepping away from damaging unconscious habits – or conditioning – lets us live more freely.

Now, please don't be disheartened, but it's suggested that full deconditioning can take seven years to achieve. That's the length of time that Saturn takes to square your birth chart *and* an average of how long it takes your body's cells to regenerate. Some cells regenerate far faster (while others may never regenerate!) and it is believed you need to decondition physically, as well as through your mind. Deconditioning is a continuous process. You'll have to go through the prompts below again, and again, but remember that life isn't linear and deconditioning *definitely* isn't either! But these *skills* are part of a toolkit you'll use forever.

Keeping a deconditioning diary will form a body of written evidence you can refer to as you explore Human Design. You will have concrete notes on your experiences, which will help you become aware of repeated patterns and damaging behaviours. Any type of journaling can bring clarity to your thoughts, improve your communication skills and build self-awareness, but your deconditioning diary will become integral to your personal Human Design toolkit. These are the elements to consider every day...

Me time

If you don't start your day with meditation, create a solo ritual that gives you a moment to be alone and undistracted. First thing is a glorious way to begin each day (but any moment can be made just for you). Stand barefoot in your garden to physically ground yourself using the earth's magnetic field; watch the clouds from your favourite chair; indulge in a little yoga. Removing yourself from 'doing' to a state of simply 'being' will help you decondition from society's 'shoulds' and obligations.

DIARY PROMPT: What would you do if you didn't have to please anyone? What would you do if you knew you couldn't fail? What gifts do you have and what skills comes naturally to you?

Activate change

Ask what part of your routine can change, each day. Drive a different route to work; stop at an alternative coffee shop;

chat to colleagues you don't usually socialise with; ask your partner different questions; mix up what you eat; experiment with different bedtime rituals. Removing yourself from living on autopilot will allow you to consider the expected actions you've been beholden to and let you *actively* choose a life that feels more right for you.

DIARY PROMPT: Where have you been today? What environments were you in and how did you feel? Who is in your social circle? Do they buoy you up, or drain you?

Process your emotions

Every action has an emotion attached to it, and in turn, every emotion has a physical feeling. Consider what you are feeling throughout the day. Are you fizzing with frustration? Do you feel tight in your temples or achy in your gut? Is your Not-Self Theme present? The more you sit with your feelings, the easier it will be to identify your body's own urges, rather than those that are conditioned – or belong to others.

DIARY PROMPT: What excited you today? What are you drawn to and what repels you?

Shadow work

In psychology, shadow work dives deep into your unconscious mind to reveal parts of your personality that you're hiding. In Human Design, allowing your shadows to breathe will help you to move on. If you ignore the shadow you'll carry on in your expected pathway, so notice how your shadows have infiltrated your life. Be warned, realising your shadows can make you feel deep grief for what could have been, but harnessing your shadows can help you create a brilliant vision for your future.

DIARY PROMPT: Where do you feel you're holding yourself back? When do you feel you've done something because you were obliged to?

Practise mindfulness

Notice when your mind starts telling you to do something – or not – or those pesky negative thought patterns return. If you are really ready to commit yourself to deep personal growth, you will need to focus on making intentional choices. Challenge the expected thinking and then go ahead and build a new neural pathway to move on. When you get it right, your body will tell you, so celebrate, and be open to gratitude, wonder and love!

DIARY PROMPT: What are you doing that you once loved – but now are bored or frustrated by?

RELEASE YOUR MIND

One of the most important concepts of Human Design is to release yourself from mind-focused thinking and using your brain for analytical decision-making, which we currently do in mainstream life. Human Design advises you to live instinctively through your energy (which will be explained in more detail in Chapter 6), so rather than using your conscious mind to make decisions, instead you go deeper, letting your Inner Authority (see page 37) take control.

Making decisions is tough. When we reach a metaphorical crossroad, our minds go into overdrive, working out the variables. We hope for the best result, but dwell on the worst outcome, which builds up so much fear and worry that it can make us physically unwell. It is why we seek other people's opinions, spend time in research and go over all the possible outcomes. But because these outcomes are always unknown, using our minds in this way leads to anxiety and self-doubt. Conversely, if you make a choice aligned to your Authority, rather than through your mind, it will always be the right choice for you and the path you are on. You will discover more about how to use your unique intuition in Chapter 6, on Authority, and how to listen to your gut or your instincts.

We are in the midst of an anxiety epidemic. Our brains are busy. Human Design believes that your mind can never guide you to your highest expression because it simply is not designed for that job. Instead, by letting your energetic Authority (which is based in your chakras) guide you in making decisions, you can release your mind so that your brain is free to create, to observe and to analyse. Being free from overthinking, decision-making and anxiety is a blessing.

Getting to the stage where you can live more freely and allow your Authority to make decisions comes through a process called deconditioning. As we go through life, we collect ideas, opinions and beliefs about how we should live. It is society's way of putting us back in our boxes. Everything from the type of home that we should live in; how our relationships should function; what a good work environment consists of; what makes us a good employee or boss. Each part of your life will have a judgement attached, based on your current conditioning. To live your Human Design, you need to start ignoring the 'should' behaviours that you have taken on board (and are likely crippled by) and live authentically as your true self, stepping back from those learned behaviours through deconditioning. Later in this book, you will encounter reminders of those 'should' behaviours that may trigger your Not-Self Theme, when you are out of alignment.

When you are beginning to live your Human Design, the next steps will see you lean into the learnings you'll discover from your unique Human Design Chart. Following Human Design alone will not allow you to decondition, that is something you must work towards yourself, but your Chart *will* reveal information about possible best practices to take you to the next step of living authentically. Human Design does not give you a rule book of commandments to follow. Living your best life according to Human Design will involve time to understand what feels true to you… and equally what does not. Sometimes it is a whole lifetime's work. As you explore your Type, Authority and Profile, different elements of your chart will make sense as you go through different situations in your life, but by removing any expectations, fears and beliefs you may have from societal conditioning, you will be well on your way to acing being an adult.

As for life's biggest questions – 'Why am I here?' and 'What is my purpose?' – take comfort that everyone is battling to know the reason why they're on this earth. You will find clues when you discover your Incarnation Cross (see page 38), which will free you from the soul-crushing search to find an answer, but know this: your purpose is not your job, or the career you are in, and you do not have to go on a quest to discover that purpose, nor do you have to change yourself to find it. You may have had a strong sense of your purpose and yourself when you were younger, although perhaps it has become blurred through conditioning and general life-ing. Knowing your Human Design is a wonderfully freeing way to gain clarity and give yourself permission to get back to the essence of you. Or, to discover it afresh, if you did not feel it earlier.

One way of thinking about your purpose is that it is not *what* you are doing, but the energy you give to everything you do. When you are confident that you are working through life's situations in accordance with your Type, your purpose will become clear. When you know how to respond to your energy and Authority with authenticity, you will start to live your purpose perfectly.

> **HOW TO RELEASE YOUR MIND**
>
> If you want to move into a more aligned plane there are two techniques you can integrate into your life, to shift your body into a more energetically-receptive place: meditation and sound healing. Try to experience one of these elements daily (although don't stress if you can't do something *every* day!).

Meditation

Possibly the most misunderstood (yet easiest) practise to incorporate, meditating will help you become aware of your thoughts without judgement. Mediation is recommended by most health services to reduce stress and is a brilliant way to start your day (although you can carve out meditation time *any* time). I suggest you set your alarm clock to wake 20 minutes earlier than usual and find a comfortable chair. Keep your legs uncrossed and rest your hands on your thighs, and as you breathe in and out, allow your mind to focus on the action of your breath.

Beginners can use an app (HeadSpace has hundreds of guided meditations to follow) or search for 'guided meditation' to find music or a practitioner you like online. By using breath-work, meditation removes the brain's normal spotlight on your thoughts and helps clear your mind so your physical body (i.e. the breath) is the focus. If your mind starts to wander, don't panic! Be aware that meditation is *not* about switching off your thoughts, you're just letting them be. Meditation helps you acknowledge your thoughts' existence without being moved to act, so you can tune into physical sensations instead and gain greater awareness of your body. This is a useful tool for your Human Design journey ahead, particularly as you learn about your Authority, which is rooted in physical sensations.

FOLLOW UP: After your meditation, jot down a few notes on the session including practical details (where you were, what you listened to, the date and time) along with any insights that came to you, the physical sensations you noticed and your feelings before and after the meditation.

Sound healing

This is a glorious way to start activating your energy centres so you can begin to feel different sensations. Sound travels through your body and resonates in certain areas where you may feel tension, heat or vibrations – this is the sound waves' frequency breaking up stuck energy. Sound healing allows you to practise tuning into your physical body to help your awareness of where and how you can listen to your Authority's guidance.

You could join a group session and sit (or lie) in circle while the practitioner leads you, or you can find a 10-minute guided meditation online (by searching: 'sound healing meditation'). It's completely normal to need to release emotion through crying, laughing or clearing your throat during – and after – sound healing.

FOLLOW UP: After each session note the different sounds used, along with the date, location and the physical sensations you noticed, as well as how you feel after the session. When you become more used to sound healing you can start each session with an intention (one example could be that you want to say no to social events that don't excite you), and then journal in your deconditioning diary to see how you feel about your goal as the days pass.

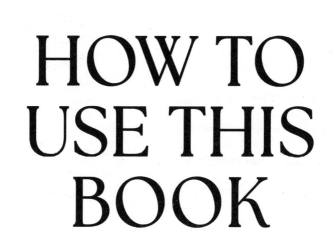

HOW TO USE THIS BOOK

HOW TO USE THIS BOOK

When I was first introduced to Human Design, I rushed to generate my Chart. I was so excited to discover the insights that lay ahead of me. When it popped up on my phone, I stared at the results for a while, then abandoned it. The lines, the shapes, the symbols, the colours, the mysterious statements... What on earth was an Incarnation Cross or a Not-Self Theme? How could an Authority help me understand my place in the world and why were all those squares and triangles joined together with stripy lines? Everything about the Human Design Chart and Body Graph looked way too complex to comprehend. I was overwhelmed and so I set it aside and carried on with my everyday life, putting the potential self-discovery there to be unlocked by the Chart to the back of my mind.

The sheer depth of information in a Human Design Chart might be enough to put some people off. It is key to remember the Chart alone is not the full picture. To use a foodie analogy, generating your Chart is like being given a pile of unlabelled, mystery ingredients for the task of cooking a meal. You might make a guess as to what the individual ingredients are through taste, smell or touch, but without labels – and indeed a recipe – your supper could be inedible. Let this guide book act as a recipe as you experiment with the Human Design ingredients in your very own kitchen. A guide is essential in order to translate the meanings found within your Human Design Chart. As well as the suggestions contained in these pages, I recommend looking at the myriad online resources and blogs dedicated to the subject. Watching Ra Uru Hu's own videos and journalling on how different variables and situations affect you as you travel through your studies will lend fascinating insight to living out your own Human Design.

HOW TO GET YOUR CHART

We cannot go anywhere without your Chart. If you have yet to get your Chart, here is how to find out who you are defined to be. All you need is your place, date and time of birth, which you can input into one of several Human Design Chart calculators online or via an app. These are some of the best-known and most-respected chart calculators:

>**JovianArchive.com** – *this site is where you will find all of Ra's teachings, writing and videos*
>**daylunalife.com**
>**myhumandesign.com**
>**puregenerators.com**
>**MyBodyGraph.com**

Inputting the exact time of your birth, right down to the minute, is key (always use the 24-hour clock) as it could have huge – although sometimes small – implications for your Chart. From experimentation, I have seen that the Profile can change throughout the day you were born but even your Type could change, depending on the time of your birth.

If you do not know, ask your parents, guardians, relatives, the local authority or the hospital where you were born. Without the exact time, your chart cannot be 100 per cent accurate because Human Design goes into minutiae of the cosmic set-up at your exact moment of birth.

If you cannot discover the exact time of your birth, however, do not panic. Astrologers can work out your birth time from a process called birth-time rectification, based on retracing your life experiences. You can also experiment by inputting various times into the Chart calculator and noticing the different elements from each time, you can then try living with the advice from each section to determine which feels more appropriate and right for you. For the most prominent elements of Human Design, you will be able to get started without knowing the minute of your birth. This book covers the most impactful elements of your Chart, with less information on the deeper-dive parts (because they do go deep). Students of Human Design can dedicate their life to trying out the finer details, so if the learnings resonate, I absolutely advise you to go ahead and move to the next stage of research.

YOUR CHART AND BODY GRAPH EXPLAINED

Once you have submitted your data, you will be presented with a Chart, (see page 2 for an example) which looks like the outline of a torso, full of squares and triangles. This is your Body Graph. Some shapes are coloured in and some left empty and there are lines running from each shape leading to numbers. Again, some of those lines are coloured in and some are not. Like an X-ray without your skeleton, this shows where your inner energies are placed.

On either side of the diagram, you will find a vertical list of symbols (representing the planets and astrological locations) assigned to numbers. The righthand column equates to your Personality and consciousness, showing the location of the planets at your birth. The left hand column is your Design side, relating to your unconscious self, and the planetary data here is generated from the date 88 days before your actual birthday, which is when the brain's neocortex is formed in the womb and a human develops cognizance.

You will also be given a series of statements and words, which we will be going into in depth in each chapter, but which can be quickly translated as the following... Remember, the first three are the most influential elements of your Human Design, so begin with them.

Type – this is how people experience your aura and how energy flows through you. Your Type gives the biggest clues as to how you exert energy and take it in from those around you and is similar in importance to your sun sign in astrology.

Strategy – linked to your Type, knowing your Strategy will help you move with ease and in alignment with your unique gifts and remind you how best to use your energy. From your Strategy you will discover how to find the most appropriate way to approach opportunities effortlessly.

Inner Authority – this is the energy that guides your decision making. Whether you are destined to follow your heart or trust your gut, your body should be making the decisions, not your mind.

Not-Self Theme – this is the feeling that you will experience when you are not living in alignment with your Human Design. When you feel this, it is a reminder to check in on how you are using your energy and a chance to make a better choice.

Signature – the opposite to your Not-Self Theme, your Signature is the wonderful feeling that the Universe will give you when you *are* on the right track.

Profile – this is your conscious and unconscious personality type, so it will explain how you appear to others, how you see yourself and your place in the world. The relevant numbers can be found after the decimal point on the Sun line of your chart. These two numbers are attached to your Profile, with the first showing your conscious traits and the second the way that others see you (your unconscious traits). They combine in a way that is unique to you.

- **Definition** – this relates to how you process new information and connect with others. Your Definition reflects how your energy centres are connected by Channels. Definition also applies to your interactions with your inner self, as well as those with others.
- **Centres** – the seemingly random squares and triangles on your Body Graph are energy centres. If they are coloured in, that means they are Defined and somewhere you will give your energy. If they are not coloured in, they are Undefined and a Centre that will take in energy from elsewhere.
- **Incarnation Cross** – this relates to your life's purpose (which *is not* your job or career) and often comes to light between the ages of 38 and 42. There are 192 possible Incarnation Crosses and it is a deep topic within Human Design.
- **Variables** – at the top of your chart, you will see four arrows which represent your Digestion, Environment, Perspective and Motivation. These are related to how your brain takes in information around it and interprets the situations you find yourself in.
- **Gates and Channels** – the numbers (Gates) on your Body Graph are linked by Channels (the lines – both coloured-in or empty), depending on where the planets were when you were born. The Gates are activated if they are coloured in and relate to how energy flows through you. If both Gates on a Channel are activated, your Channel will be Defined and this is a way that Human Design will reveal your unique set of gifts.

Aura – this is the way your energy communicates and holds all the information from our Centres, Gates and Channels. Because your aura extends around 1.2 metres (4 feet) around your body, every time you are in close proximity to others, your auras will be communicating. You can also pick up on auras through others' words, on video calls or through online communication. Different Types have different auras.

Keep your Chart close by as you read on. You will get the most benefit from this book when you fold back pages relevant to you and jot down notes in the margins. If it feels wrong to treat a book in this way, you can start practising deconditioning! Once you know your Chart, flip straight to the sections that apply to your Type, Strategy and Authority. When you have generated Charts for others, you can read their sections exclusively too.

When you live according to your Strategy and Authority, so many other elements of living your most authentic life will flow to you, which is why these sections are covered so thoroughly in this book. To understand the most prominent themes within your Human Design, read through the chapters in order before progressing to the chapter on Next-Level Learning, for when you are ready to deep dive. Beyond This Book gives ideas on how to explore Human Design at leisure over the rest of your life. In fact, taking your time over your self-discovery is the best way to experience – and live – your most aligned life.

THE SCIENCE PART

Perhaps Human Design is now so widely accepted because of its inclusion of scientific elements. It does not rely on unseen magic or intangible beliefs and, as New Age systems go, Human Design is pragmatic. When the pull of the moon is enough to influence the tides on Earth, it is equally feasible that our energies are influenced by cosmic patterns. There are, of course, critics who argue that Human Design has no evidence-based scientific verification to back up the genetic and astrophysical claims, but the 'a-ha' moments from realization – and sense of relief – are more than enough for the system's followers when they begin to unravel their Charts.

The finding from Ra Uru Hu that neutrinos *do* have mass, years before physicists confirmed this, is a positive tick for Human Design's credibility. A key way to view Human Design is to appreciate that the cosmic information stream that was imprinted on us at birth (and before) via neutrinos is the force that gives each and every one of us our unique energy. No other self-awareness system uses physics or quantum mechanics in the same way as Human Design. Conversely, perhaps this is a reason many might initially be put off by the system. Whereas esoteric thoughts can be easily dismissed, too deep a scientific element can confuse potential students hoping for more intuitive methodology. (But hang on, that is part of Human Design too!)

Human Design suggests that we all experience behaviours and emotions in waves, which echo the manner particles switch their properties, depending on their circumstances. This is called wave-particle duality and Human Design is said to reflect this, as humans have primary and secondary elements and everything in Human Design has two opposing sides (for example our Signature and Not-Self). The 64 gates in your Body Graph also correspond with the 64 hexagrams in the I Ching and the 64 codons that make up human DNA, but again this seems more anecdotal than firmly based in science.

Beyond physics, Human Design also brings in elements of psychology and personality testing. The Types, Centres and Gates you will read about shortly have parallels with Jungian psychology and psychological profiling. There may never be a conclusive study to confirm the actuality and efficacy of Human Design, but any methods that we can use to reach deeper self-realization and acceptance can surely only ever impact positively on our existence.

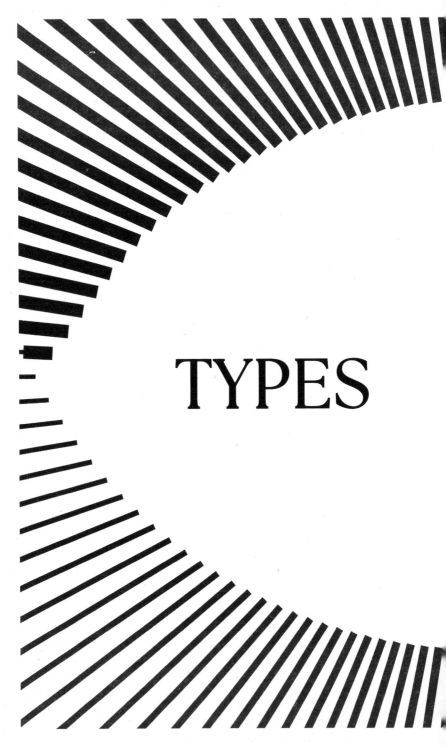
TYPES

TYPES

Your unique Type is the biggest element in defining your Human Design – it's like your sun sign in Astrology. There are five types and each exerts energy – and takes it in – in different ways. This flow of energy influences how other people will experience your presence and aura. Knowing your Type will give you ideas on how to manage your energy, work flow and relationships. Go straight to read about your Type first and then read the sections on those around you to gain greater clarity on how you can optimise your relationships.

My Type is

_____

GENERATOR

WHO? 37% of the population
STRATEGY: Wait to respond
AURA: Open and enveloping
SIGNATURE: Satisfaction
NOT-SELF THEME: Frustration

GENERATOR GIFTS

Being a Generator in alignment is like being plugged into the mains. You could light up the world with your energy. If you have ever lost track of time, doing something you love, but still felt like you could continue all night, that is a classic Generator trait. Generator's sacral centres are defined, so not only do you have a consistent energy bank for yourself, but you can also power those around you. It is exhilarating to be so close to such enthusiasm, but Generators need to practise saying 'no'. People may try to take advantage of your energy or you could expend too much of your life force on tasks that aren't aligned for you, which can lead to burnout and your Not-Self Theme of frustration.

The most important learning for a Generator is to listen to your gut. Your gut aligns to your sacral centre and this is the most significant part of your Chart. It is where your energy flows from. As a Generator, you need to decondition from brain-led decision-making and follow your body's desires. Think about all the decisions you take each day. Notice how your gut feels for each decision made, rather than what your brain thinks. When your gut contracts, if you feel your battery drain or sigh inside, it is your body's way of saying that it is not right to get involved. Whenever you feel excitement expanding from deep within your belly, those are the things to say 'yes' to. As that energy emanates from your body, through your aura, that is when life will bring you the most exciting opportunities. Your responses might change over time, but if it is not a 'hell yeah!', then it is a 'no'. Move away from saying 'yes' just because it is the 'right' thing to do or you *think* it will lead to a positive result.

Concentrating on the most positive opportunities is the route to living your Signature of satisfaction and increasing your magnetism. Although sometimes there *are* tasks that you need to get through, despite your gut contracting (cleaning the bathroom, for example), noticing your response will still bolster your magnetism to opportunities that will lead to greater satisfaction.

Consistency is your buzz word. Generators have a steady energy flow and the stamina to complete tasks but find it hard to stop or pivot. Likewise, you can be prone to burnout if you are not doing tasks that tick your Signature of satisfaction. Leave free time in your diary to make space for your body to tell you what excites you, to give you more aligned opportunities. 'When one door closes, a window opens with a better view.' The universe is always ready to fill an empty space with something better. You might feel you need to be busy to be successful, but it is better for Generators to do nothing than a task that does not inspire.

Day to day, a Generator needs to eat when they are hungry, not when their brain says it is mealtime. Only consume what you feel you need. Focusing on your sacral guidance will ensure you are taking in the right nourishment, whether that is one of your five-a-day or a little treat. You do not need time to unwind and can head straight to bed when you are tired, but you should go to sleep feeling satisfied with your day, drained but happy and ready to go again tomorrow. You need to use up all your energy doing things you really love, rather than tasks that lead to frustration, otherwise you could feel depressed at bedtime.

Unfulfilled Generators will try to expend energy somewhere else, so be careful to not allow frustration to develop into an adrenalin-chasing search for satisfaction through gambling or another addiction. Generators often worry about what's coming next, again becoming frustrated. Your inner guidance works in the now and your sacral centre knows when you should do something - or not - but only the universe knows how it will end up, so practise releasing your worries.

GENERATORS AT WORK

Generators have a unique way to make visions reality through hard work and skill, but they need to love their work, whether self-employed or part of a team, otherwise they'll get frustrated. Consistency and tenacity are key words for Generators. You will work steadily until you are at the top of your game, then once you are there, you will wonder how you did it. Generators have a hard time noticing their own brilliance.

The best way for a Generator to build success is to find something you love and your passion will draw people to you, rather than deciding on a business to fill a gap in the market. However brilliant your idea is – and it *will* be brilliant – it is *you* that your customers will buy into, not your service. Your Generator life force has a knock-on effect and spreads energy to your colleagues, making them more productive too.

You want to fulfil all your tasks immaculately. Generators have an inner quest for mastery and you always commit wholeheartedly. As you are learning, you sometimes reach a plateau where you can consolidate your skills before moving higher. That is natural, just be aware that these moments can trigger your conditioning to worry about what's next. Do not give into frustration over what you perceive as slow progress. Just wait. Your next batch of energy will come when you are ready to move on. If you continue to be at a low ebb, it is likely you are on the wrong path and so wait for the right opportunity instead of pushing. Remember your Strategy is to respond, not force action.

Even when you do not want to do something, you will give it your all. Others might notice your expansive energy bank and set you endless tasks, however, you must remember that you are not meant to work without passion. Listen to your gut and say 'no' to tasks that do not spark enthusiasm to protect you from burnout and reach your Signature of satisfaction. Feeling satisfied is a cozy, expansive glow that the universe wants you to experience all the time. When you say 'yes' to everything, your energy drains quickly. When you do energizing work, as a Generator, you will actually have more energy!

Move on from conditioned thoughts about fame, success, wealth or material goods. It is a myth that you will never make money doing something you love, so ignore your mind's belief that you need to make a long-term plan. Instead, live in the present, which is aligned to your truth. Do not get hung up on chasing dreams, scouting opportunities or pushing for meetings. Make sure your unique skills are visible (update your LinkedIn profile or polish up your CV), then carry on the momentum until the time is right to respond.

GENERATORS AND PEOPLE

Your inviting aura means you draw people into your circle and others describe you as warm, welcoming and nurturing. Generators instantly connect with others and understand who needs support. However, just because your aura is open, it does not mean you should always help whenever you are asked. While your default is to say 'yes', sacrificing yourself for the sake of others and doing things that do not excite you will deplete your energy. Remind yourself that your life force needs to be protected to ensure your energy is directed towards doing what you actually love. Remove the conditioning that this is selfish behaviour.

Doing something for somebody else that does not light your fire may elicit praise, so you *think* it is a good thing, but praise is a conditioned reaction and not linked to your purpose or energy. Generators need to stop always putting others first.

Do not go to the party if you do not want to. Do not worry about letting people down. You do not need outside validation to make decisions and instead cultivate belief in valuing your time and energy within every relationship.

In love, you need to desire a partner. Even if they are your type on paper, it does not mean they are right for you. There will be a deep sacral expansion and your Signature of satisfaction when you are with the right person. In turn, the right partner will understand and support your energy, which will lead to further satisfaction.

Generators need 'yes' and 'no' options (rather than open-ended questions). Support a Generator friend by joining them in activities they love and help them decipher what they are frustrated by. When Generators give energy through satisfaction, it is sparkling and beautiful. You do not know how special you are.

Famous generators

* Albert Einstein
* The Dalai Lama
* Elvis Presley
* Margaret Thatcher
* Oprah Winfrey
* Walt Disney

Checklist of needs for generators

* *Over the next month, ask how your body feels about every scenario you face. Can you act on those feelings?*
* *Check in with your gut over small decisions or tasks in order to practise understanding your response to bigger questions.*
* *Evaluate your daily to-do list and remove any tasks that do not excite you, so you can make space for opportunities to flow to you.*
* *Consider one option at a time to avoid confusion. Ask colleagues to present questions with 'yes' or 'no' options, to make your decisions easier to decipher.*
* *Notice when you are having trouble saying 'no'. Remember, prioritizing your own desires over others is not inherently selfish or less important.*
* *If you have a nighttime skincare routine, do it earlier in the evening before you become exhausted so that you can honour your Generator needs around sleep.*
* *Open up your throat centre by singing, which will help to vocalize your sacral sounds.*
* *Find a hobby that you love and make time for fun – you do not need to always be busy to be successful.*

Crystal kit for generators

* Citrine will increase your magnetism and confidence and give your creativity a boost.
* Carnelian is aligned with your sacral chakra, so will help to kick-start and energize projects.
* Sunstone will amplify your Generator radiance and remind you of your true worth.

Essential oils for generators

✸ Clove, cinnamon, lemon and vetiver.

Affirmations for generators

✸ I trust my gut feeling to know when something is right for me to pursue, even if I cannot visualize the next step.
✸ My energy and time are precious and so I say 'no' to anything that is not aligned to my purpose.
✸ Spending my days doing tasks that fill me with joy and excitement will lead to greater abundance.

MANIFESTING GENERATOR

WHO? 33% of the population
STRATEGY: Wait to respond
AURA: Open and enveloping
SIGNATURE: Satisfaction and peace
NOT-SELF THEME: Frustration and anger

MANIFESTING GENERATOR GIFTS

A perfect blend of Manifestor and Generator energy, as a Manifesting Generator you create energy through doing what excites you. You are blessed with a dynamic combination of Manifestor spontaneity and Generator consistency. I recommend you read both the Manifestor and Generator descriptions to understand how these two energies merge within you.

The two elements of your Type blend to give Manifesting Generators (often abbreviated to MGs) a unique ability to jump into action, although you need to live your Strategy to wait to respond (rather than act immediately) to ensure you have the energy to carry out any tasks. MGs live life in top gear and are multi-hyphenate success stories. However, learning patience and noticing your feelings in every moment will help you to avoid the mistakes that can sometimes affect your speedy approach to tasks.

You have a defined sacral centre, which provides you with a life force that powers you and those around you, plus a connection to the throat chakra. MGs have an open aura. Are you always asked to help or advise others, but have trouble saying 'no'? When faced with tasks that you do not want to do, they'll drain your energy, leading you to sacrifice yourself through burnout. It is not selfish or unkind to say 'no'. Just because you can take on a task (and you *can* do everything, and at speed, too), you still need to protect your energy and only do tasks that spark your interest. Making space by removing obligations that do not excite you will allow more aligned opportunities to flow to you.

Your response to a question may change at a later date, but right now, which is the timeframe your sacral centres understand, it is a 'no' if your gut contracts, you feel an internal sigh or vocalize an external 'no'. Sometimes you will be faced with elements that are not an immediate, definite 'no', but equally if they're not a clear 'yes', it is still a 'no'. These 'meh' situations are the biggest energy drains for MGs. If you love your career and work, but often feel frustrated and tired, consider where these energy leaks could be. Living according to your Human Design requires you to notice what you feel and what fires you, what expands your gut with excitement... Then you need to go and do it!

MGs are creative geniuses. Innovators and inventors, you are the Type that will work out a shortcut that could change the world. You attract people who want you to be part of *their* visions and your aura is highly receptive. You bring contagious energy and passion to the world although you do have a note of unpredictability to your life through your spontaneous energy pattern. MGs are not built to stick to a rule book or make plans for next year, now. Your passions aren't random. The universe has put them in your orbit for a reason and when you do things you love, the universe will reward you with more energy.

Your aptitude for pivoting comes from your connection between the sacral centre and throat and, in any process, you understand how to be better and faster. You pick up new skills through an energy surge of mastery and, while you might not use those learnings immediately, know that one day it will make sense. Luckily, MGs love exploration, adventure and the excitement of the unknown.

Each day, ask what your body feels about everything in front of you. Can you honour your gut response? Sometimes it is not possible, but even acknowledging the feeling will start to build up your magnetism to things that *are* aligned. MGs often need to slow down and wait to respond. Trust that your body will tell you what's right and move beyond your mind telling whether something is a good idea.

Sometimes MGs need bigger portions of food, or to eat more often, to sustain their energy. Go to bed with an empty energy bank, satisfied with how you spent your day. Aim for healthy exhaustion not anxious, unfulfilled feelings that there is more to be done. After 10pm you may get a second wind, which means you stay up after you are tired, so try to go to bed early and read or listen to a podcast to help you wind down. Even though your days might be jam-packed, leave space for the universe to fill any gaps.

MGs are the Type to break out from boxes that society has built and expand the entire human perspective through their genius and innovation. You will defy all preconceived ideas and guide everyone into the future with brilliance and vision, forging a completely new path.

MANIFESTING GENERATORS AT WORK

Ignore the conditioned thought that you need to work in a linear manner for success. MGs should work in any manner they like. The freedom to shift will be key to your satisfaction. Sticking with an unexciting task until you finish will only lead to frustration, so if you are not passionate, leave it and replace it with a more energizing activity. If you are worried about people thinking you are fickle or lacking in focus, remember experimentation is part of your MG mission.

You may have a mundane job, but your Type has the boundary-pushing knowledge and urge to improve or streamline dull tasks, making them more efficient and even fun. Your employer, employees and colleagues need to allow you the freedom to experiment and invent shortcuts. If you feel the need to explore another area of work, do not let your conditioned mind – or others – tell you it is not logical or a good idea. You need to expand and always explore the tasks that fire you up. An MG needs stimulus to create your Signature of satisfaction.

You are the person people come to for advice on better methods and hacks because MGs can do many things, all at once. Whether that is juggling different careers or building a side hustle, because you are adept at so many tasks, you have the patience and wait to respond. When you have many tasks, which you are doing at speed, your brain can start thinking about the next steps. Remember to be in the moment to enjoy the process and focus. You can sometimes skip ahead and miss important elements, which will lead to frustration, a stuck sensation or real anger.

Even though you can work hard, you are not on this planet to labour. Narrow down your tasks to those you love, they will make the biggest difference to your life flow and the entire planet.

MANIFESTING GENERATORS AND PEOPLE

Freedom is key for MGs in any relationship. You have a need to experience everything you want in love and friendship, although sometimes you forget to remind those around you of an impending pivot. If you feel your intentions are often misunderstood, consider whether you are communicating enough (practise opening your throat chakra through singing) and ensure you always inform your loved ones when you are about to do something.

Avoid acting before you are ready, as this will drain your energy and trigger burnout. It might seem like a good idea in your head, or perhaps you have been advised to act now, but it is essential you listen to your Strategy of waiting to respond. That does not mean slowly thinking about an answer, the response comes from your inner sacral centre, your belly, which with either expand with positivity or contract with an internal headshake.

While your partners do not need physically to keep up with your incredible MG speed, they do need to respect you and provide space for you to do your own thing. You often build strong relationships around activities and projects that inspire you, so find a hobby that you can share with friends. Engaging with a hobby you love will also use up any excess energy. Everyone you surround yourself with should lift you up and energize you, just as your unique energy does to those you invite into your circle. Use your family, friends and partners to help you narrow down the options by asking 'yes' or 'no' questions to work out what you want and identify the next steps.

If you feel your Not-Self Theme of frustration emerging in any relationship, ask yourself what are you afraid of changing and what would you like to explore? You need to get involved with your desires, so inform those around you so they know what's coming. Your inviting aura means that opportunities will come to you, so you never need to chase connections, whether at work or in relationships.

Famous manifesting generators

* Angelina Jolie
* David Beckham
* Dr Martin Luther King Jr
* Miley Cyrus
* Mother Teresa
* Stephen King

Checklist of needs for manifesting generators

* *Ensure you have something in your life right now that energizes you, whether a big or small project.*
* *Make sure you do not slip into frustration, or anger, by doing tasks you are not energized by and note what makes you feel tired and frustrated.*
* *Quitting is not a sign of weakness. The universe gives an MG permission to move on to what energizes you.*
* *Make sure you have people around you who respect your need for freedom. In return, you must communicate your needs with them.*
* *Always take time to wind down and relax before bed, heading to sleep in peaceful satisfaction.*
* *Create space between your various ventures with different workplaces, brands, websites or social media profiles.*
* *Be aware when you are being blocked from your true needs, whether that is in relationships, work, friendships or creatively.*
* *Be present and make even the most mundane tasks a ritual of mindfulness.*

Crystal kit for manifesting generators

* Chrysocolla will help you speak your truth, particularly when you need to tell others your plans.
* Amethyst is ideal when you are living at high speed and need to wind down and calm yourself.
* Black tourmaline is a protective stone to help you move away from societal conditioning.

Essential oils for manifesting generators

* Tangerine, cinnamon, lavender and chamomile.

Affirmations for manifesting generators

* The right opportunities flow to me when I am present and listen to my Inner Authority.
* When something no longer excites me, I move on without guilt.
* I dedicate my precious energy to tasks that light me up.

MANIFESTOR

WHO? 9% of the population
STRATEGY: To inform
AURA: Selective, closed and impactful
SIGNATURE: Peace
NOT-SELF THEME: Anger

MANIFESTOR GIFTS

Manifestors are wild, spontaneous characters who love to live freely and the universe gives you permission to do whatever you want. You receive energy through urges – divine messages – from the universe, unlike the other Types who must wait or tap into their sacral desires to get energy. Manifestor energy is inconsistent. You can work non-stop 24/7 on a task you love, but then need a week off to recover. Ask how you are feeling every day to honour the energy that fizzes to start new projects or unplug when you need rest to prepare for your next energetic burst.

You are on this earth to inspire and your Human Design makes you extremely independent. You continuously spark ideas and, while people flock to you, some will be repelled by your plans and other will not even notice... but do not worry about them. Your selective aura will bring the right people to join you and leave the wrong ones in the dust.

If you have wondered where your ideas and urges come from, these sudden desires are gifts from the universe. They're given to you as an initiator or a catalyst. As soon you receive an urge, say it out loud to inspire others to run with it. Although if an urge keeps coming back, consider if it is something that *you* should take on.

Your Strategy to inform means speaking out loud. Tell everyone your plans *before* you do them and the world will have your back. Manifestors' Strategy does not come naturally. You would rather be left alone, but as your aura is closed you need to tell people your plans. No-one can guess your next step. If you ever feel misunderstood, living your Strategy of informing will improve this sensation. Whether you are craving alone time, popping to the shops or struggling to get excited at work, nothing is too small to share. If you feel unsupported, consider if you informed the people around you. Or did you inform them too late?

Sometimes Manifestor energy is mistaken for loudness or aggression. Remember that Manifestors are larger-than-life people because you have big ideas to share with the world. Never apologize for your boldness. Live unapologetically and the right people will notice you, but check in to see if you have any fear around being seen. Try journalling to remove that fear.

Manifestors can struggle to fit into society's boxes, shrinking themselves to avoid drama and becoming people pleasers. Conversely, sometimes they break out of societal constraints and rebel wildly. Criticism makes you want to hide, but accepting your unique gifts will bring untold abundance.

Freedom is key for you. You have a fear of being controlled. Everyone wants to know what your next step is, but as your aura is protective and repelling, it can make people wary of you, too. Your sweet spot is where you can respect those around you and inform them of your plans, while still honouring your own desires.

A Manifestor's aura is an amplifier and your words and actions have the power to literally manifest your desires into reality. Often you have no idea that your words are such powerful catalysts of change in others' lives. You lead unintentionally.

At the end of the day, go to bed before you are tired and spend an hour settling your energy before you sleep. As a Manifestor, you need to eat what you want, when you want and exercise however you want. Eating according to others' plans could trigger problems with your digestion while the wrong exercise will drain you.

Whether you are building a small community in your village or spearheading a worldwide movement, your presence as a Manifestor will resonate far and wide.

MANIFESTORS AT WORK

Manifestors have inconsistent energy patterns, so even if you love your job, working nine to five could exhaust you, unless you have a healthy work/life balance and freedom from your boss. Often Manifestors find success in self-employment. Whenever you feel stifled, it is time to move on. You need space in your schedule to create what suits you.

Take time to consider where you are holding back in work. Where are you afraid to show up as your authentic self? When you are living in alignment, you will notice before problems arise so that you will never get backed into a corner (and become angry). Sometimes people will not like your plans. It can be scary sharing big-picture ideas that might be rejected, but it is your duty to do it. As you learn to understand your aura, you will realize that you cannot please everyone all the time. It might be helpful to remember rejection is not personal, it is simply an exchange of energies.

However, do not forget your Strategy to inform. This will allow those around you to adjust to your ideas and get ready for changes, so when they know your feelings, they will support you. If you hit resistance or misunderstanding, you could become angry, ranging from mild annoyance to full-blown fury. When you feel fatigue or burnout yourself, the solution is to inform some more. Try to understand why your Not-Self Theme of anger has emerged so you are better placed to manage it.

You are the ideas person at work and should share every urge you have. Manifestors are often leaders or run their own companies; you have epic ideas and need a trusted team to bring them to life. Received thought says you should start a task and see it through to completion, but Manifestors need to move on when called to something new. Never push harder to get through an energy dip when you are ready to move on. You do not need to prove you can do it all. Release the guilt and trust others. Controlling behaviour and micromanagement can breed resentment, so allow other people to run with your ideas. You can become a brilliant leader with your Manifestor gifts.

Societal requirements also demand that you have all the answers for a new idea immediately. Remove the worry about sharing ideas before they are 'ready'. Your role as a Manifestor is not to sweat the small stuff. Trust that the answers will come when you need them.

MANIFESTORS AND PEOPLE

Before living in alignment, a Manifestor may live a lonely existence because your aura is closed. It might feel hard at times, but this keeps you safe from others' energy and enables you to live your own truth. Your closed aura stops others from reading you and protects you from outside influences. Some people are physically repelled by your aura, while others are inspired by you and attracted to you. Others' energetic reactions will decide who is aligned to you – or not – to ensure your circle is authentic. Sometimes you doubt you will ever find your people, but the universe will bring an army of allies to you, who will adore you for exactly who you are.

If you have ever been told that you are 'too much', ignore those opinions. Your truest friends will support you whenever you share your urges. Your boldest self might be told off for causing drama, when all you want is peace, but however tempting it might be, never hide. Your friends and family might not be able to keep up with your energy, but they do need to support your intensity because you can move mountains when you are in energetic flow.

You need to take the lead in relationships, which can be scary, but living your Strategy of informing future partners of your desires and sharing your truth is essential. Receiving equal support, having enough alone-time and considerate communication are green flags in your relationships.

Being controlled is your worst nightmare and can result in your Not-Self Theme of anger. Sometimes anger can turn inwards and materialize as depression, burnout or people-pleasing. The goal is not to remove your Not-Self Theme from your Human Design as we need these signs to keep us on the right track. Never think of your Not-Self Theme as 'bad', it is just a reminder to head back into your Signature.

As you go through life, you will impact everyone in your path, whether you realize or not, so when you are informing, remain compassionate. The universe does not want you to hurt people and your urges are always for the highest good. Knowing you have a polarizing aura will let you move towards peace.

Famous manifestors

* Adele
* Al Gore
* Bruce Springsteen
* George W. Bush
* Gloria Steinem
* Jennifer Aniston
* Maya Angelou

Checklist of needs for manifestors

* *List ten positive things about yourself and say them out loud to yourself in the mirror each morning.*
* *Pay attention to your urges.*
* *Find an outlet for when you feel anger (such as shouting into a pillow), then evaluate the situation around the anger, to see if you can stop the feeling repeating itself.*
* *Note the people in your life you experience friction with and work out if there is a way you can inform them more.*
* *When you need to make a change, write down every person you need to inform and tell them.*
* *Listen to when your body guides you towards rest and set boundaries around alone time.*
* *Ask when you felt at your most peaceful each day.*
* *Notice potential problems to help you remain in charge of your own life and not become controlled by any person or circumstance.*

Crystal kit for manifestors

* Citrine to help activate your Inner Authority and manifest your dreams.
* Black tourmaline will protect you against outside opinions, influences and negative energy.
* Rose quartz will allow you to feel compassion when informing all those around you.

Essential oils for manifestors

* Spearmint, cardamom, sandalwood and geranium.

Affirmations for manifestors

* Being unapologetically me will always allow me to impact the right people.
* I trust the urges I receive to guide my actions towards showing the world a better way to be and do.
* My unique voice will inform and inspire those in my circle and beyond to bring me peace.

PROJECTOR

WHO? 20% of the population
STRATEGY: Wait for the invitation
AURA: Focused and penetrating
SIGNATURE: Success
NOT-SELF THEME: Bitterness

PROJECTOR GIFTS

You are here to guide others by sharing your expertise and insights with the world. You have so much knowledge to bestow, however, you can only share these gifts when someone is ready – hence your Strategy to wait for the invitation. Waiting can lead to frustration and your Not-Self Theme of bitterness (although you can counteract this by building self-love) but know this: all Projectors are destined for wild success. It is your Signature.

Your aura, which defines your Type, is focused and penetrating, which means you can reach deep into other people's auras to see them *and* the truth in a situation, whether that is things they are struggling with or undiscovered talents. You are particularly perceptive and have a unique perspective on every situation. You can also see the steps others should take to become the best versions of themselves. You can offer your help if someone asks for it and it is okay to remind people, 'I am here for you', but do not go around sharing unsolicited advice. This is partly to protect your energy, but also because Projectors need to know that their gifts will be truly appreciated before they share them. Being an observer is your superpower. Projectors are often described as having a birds-eye view of a situation, as you can clearly see the patterns and mistakes playing out in front of you.

Projectors are non-energy beings, as your sacral centre is undefined, which means your energy dips. You take in energy from the people around you because you cannot create your own. Projectors are renowned for loving sleep and do need plenty of rest. You are unlikely to thrive in a typical nine-to-five work environment, but your skillset means Projectors become wonderful leaders, because you can guide others in their own energetic journeys.

As your energy patterns fluctuate so much, aim for 10 hours of sleep a night and remove the conditioning we have all received about the 'best' ways to work. You do not need to be 'doing' all day. Try focusing on a task for 3–4 hours, then rest, read, research or do 'easier' tasks for the rest of the day. Projectors crave recognition of their genius and can slip into the Not-Self Theme of bitterness if they do not receive it. Remember that acknowledging your brilliance starts with you. As a Projector, you need to see the brilliance in yourself, just as you do with everyone else.

PROJECTORS AT WORK

Your purpose is to guide others, so Projectors make excellent leaders. You are likely to really care about efficiency pathways to make work easier. Working smarter, not harder should be your goal. While Projectors can work anywhere and be an expert in any number of fields, you will do best focusing on areas where you can share your valuable skills and wisdom. Even though you do not thrive in traditional workplace conditions, Projectors often place career ahead of everything and will be a success in all that you do, although success means so many things to different people.

When you put yourself out there, you are destined to be recognized for your talent and gifts, but if you have fallen for the myth of the hustle and feel you constantly need to be 'doing' to be successful, that will not work for you. You will slide into your Not-Self Theme of bitterness, so be aware of when this happens to realign yourself and get back to living your true Human Design to allow your Signature success to be.

Projectors often suit one-to-one work situations and might feel overwhelmed when many people are talking at them. Sometimes you feel that to get things done, you need to do it all yourself. Remember to decondition yourself by knowing that *doing* is not your benchmark of success and fill your day with tasks that fascinate you, rather than those you feel you 'should' be doing.

Some Projectors may diagnose themselves with the traits of a Highly Sensitive Person, as identified by Elaine Aron, and become overwhelmed by bright lights, sudden noises or intense smells and need to create strong boundaries. Even though you do not have the same energy reserves as other types, know that you will always have enough energy to be successful in the right areas for you.

One tip for Projectors: do not offer your advice for free. This is often true in creative industries where there is an expectation that you can contribute your skills for exposure, but that is not okay. You should share your gifts only with those who truly appreciate you and recognize your talent. It just might take a little longer to land your dream job. Instead of applying for roles, networking is key for Projectors. Invitations may come from people you know or have worked with rather than filling in job applications. While you are waiting for that invitation, do not just sit around. It is not code for passiveness. You could build a website or create social media posts that advertise your skills or arrange coverage in the media about your business.

Projectors harvest energy from the people that surround them and the transits of the planets, but because this energy mainly comes from others, you can become tired in the workplace so remember that 'no' is a complete sentence. Say it regularly when you are overwhelmed, tired and need a re-set.

PROJECTORS AND PEOPLE

Your talent for reading others means you have huge resources of empathy, but this can sometimes drain you. Remember that you cannot fix everyone or solve the problems of the world, however much you want to.

You might have taken on the role of your family and friends' unofficial therapist, but even if you have received an invitation, do not share too much. You cannot pour from an empty cup and need to feel appreciated for your advice. Likewise, offering your opinions to everyone might mean your advice falls on deaf ears (which is a waste of your precious energy) or you insult someone. As with every element of your life, set strict boundaries and rest. This can be hard with a partner, or friends, who constantly want to 'do' things but anyone in your circle needs to understand and respect that you will take your own time and are on your own path.

Do not get caught up in waiting for invitations and wondering when they will come – you will fall into your Not-Self theme of bitterness – and never worry about what other people think of you. Cultivate confidence and self-love first to set every relationship up for success. A little reminder that even if you receive an invitation, it might not be the right one. Check in to whether you feel that you gel with the other person and they truly appreciate your gifts, whether in love or friendship. If you do not, they are not the right people for you.

A WORD ON MANIFESTATION

While it is completely possible to manifest your true desires, something that is key and yet sometimes forgotten is that you need to act, too. This is where Human Design can step in to guide you. It is all very well dreaming of buying a house by the seaside, but if you have not saved enough for a deposit, your own property is not on the market and you are not spending your weekends viewing potential houses, your dream will remain out of reach.

As a Projector, you need to increase your magnetism, so that your unique skills are reaching the right audience. While you need to wait for the invitation, spend time focusing on tasks you enjoy, working out what needs improvement, building your future plans and making sure you can be seen. Recognizing and celebrating your own talents is also essential for Projectors to amplify your magnetism and allow abundance and success to flow to you. Imposter syndrome be gone.

Famous projectors

* Barack Obama
* Diana, Princess of Wales
* Jeff Bezos
* Mick Jagger
* Nelson Mandela
* Queen Elizabeth II
* Taylor Swift

Checklist of needs for projectors

* *Schedule in downtime during your day, whether that is making a cup of tea and drinking it undisturbed, walking in nature or journalling your instinctive thoughts and feelings.*
* *Rest before you get tired and ensure you have a wind-down period before bed. A warm bath is an ideal ritual before sleep.*
* *Trying sleeping alone, if you are in a relationship, particularly when you are overwhelmed and need space.*
* *Exercise lightly with low-impact yoga, stretching or swimming, rather than high-impact running or HIIT sessions.*
* *Focus on one task at a time. As a Projector, you are at risk of burnout if you take on too much.*
* *Do what fascinates you every day, rather than what you feel you should be doing.*
* *Compliment yourself on your skills, knowledge and gifts. You do not need outside validation. From self-love will flow success.*
* *Work on making your business offering clearly visible to attract invitations. You need to be seen.*

Crystal kit for projectors

* Malachite will protect against negative energy and allow you to be seen through transformation.
* Fluorite will help with focus during your 2–4 intensive hours of hard work.
* Turquoise will aid communication, whether around your boundaries or when sharing your knowledge.

Essential oils for projectors

* Rose, lavender, bergamot and myrrh.

AFFIRMATIONS FOR PROJECTORS

* My guidance, gifts and knowledge are precious. I will share them only with those who truly appreciate my energy.
* By living authentically, I will attract the best people into my energy.
* I instinctively know when authentic invitations have entered my life.

REFLECTOR

WHO? 1% of the population
STRATEGY: Wait a lunar cycle
AURA: Resistant and sampling
SIGNATURE: Surprise
NOT-SELF THEME: Disappointment

REFLECTOR GIFTS

Reflectors might make up a tiny percentage of humans, but your power and potential are limitless. Your Chart does not have defined Centres, and as you do not have an internal motor, you are a non-energy being. Instead, you take in energy from the cosmic set-up and from everyone around you. You have an intuitive perspective that allows you to understand every other type *and* experience the entire range of human behaviour, albeit temporarily. Reflectors are literal mirrors. Everyone around you sees themselves reflected in you, along with the state of the wider world, too.

As you are profoundly empathetic, you need to take regular breaks from people and situations to return to your neutral state. Have you ever been told you are too sensitive? Despite conditioned thought, your empathy and sensitivity are your greatest qualities.

Your Strategy is to wait a lunar cycle – a full 28 days – before you make any major decisions. Other Types are connected to the sun's energy, however Reflectors are lunar beings. As the moon goes through different stages, it transmits different energetic qualities, which you feel deeply. Before you decide on life-changing decisions like moving house, accepting a job offer or moving in with a partner, allow the moon to transit through your 64 gates so that you have experienced all its energies. Depending on the phase of the lunar cycle, different qualities arise in you, which means you will experience different layers of truth that will lead you to the right answer. Try journalling how you feel over the next 28 days to give you more confidence in discovering your own emotions and tapping into your lunar authority.

Waiting a month might seem impossible, but sitting with that timescale allows you to connect more deeply with yourself and cultivate life-changing patience. The universe's divine timing will always support you. Remember, your Strategy relates to life-changing decisions. The big stuff. You do not need to wait to decide whether to switch your morning latte for a mocha. With smaller decisions, go with what feels good now, although know that clarity (even over your coffee order) arrives after 28 days.

Feeling confused about your place in the world is something that affects Reflectors. As does feeling invisible at times. Just because you lack defined centres, remember that Type is only one element of your Human Design. Although your energy shifts every day, your Profile, Gates and Incarnation Cross are all consistent. Learning about these will help you to define yourself. Just because you flow through different energies each day, you are still entirely your own person.

Each morning gives you the chance to sample a new version of yourself. This freedom helps you live in your Signature of surprise. Although everyone's energy affects you, you do not solely take it in or transmit it. Your aura is discerning and resistant to negative energies. You are not just a conduit and you have the power to choose what you take in. The world can be chaotic. When you see injustice, imbalance or wrongdoing, you feel a powerful need to correct it and you have the power, resilience and strength to make better choices. Sometimes Reflectors can benefit from therapy to unpick trauma or negative thought patterns and remove them from your life.

You sometimes swing between not knowing who you are and over-identifying with people and things. There is so much pressure to pick a path but know that *your* path is to choose many paths. Received thought says we must be one type of person, forever. 'We should stay in our own lanes'. But Reflectors can be anything they like! The universe has allowed you to choose and never be backed into a box. The more you work to decondition yourself, and align with your Human Design, the more your unique persona will come to light.

Reflectors need alone time in nature, particularly when you have been around high-energy Types. You might feel wildly energized, but still need to rest. Go to bed before you are exhausted and give yourself an hour to clear the energy you have collected throughout the day. Journal about your emotions to release the day's energy and create a calming pre-sleep, wind-down routine. Reflectors sometimes sleep better solo. During the day, eat alone whenever possible. You are taking in nourishment from food *and* from those around you.

If solo dining is not possible, sit with considered eaters. Who you surround yourself with will impact your future. Embrace every one of your rare sensitivities and listen to how your body communicates to you through your skin, digestion, sleep and mood.

The Not-Self Theme for Reflectors is disappointment; a creeping sadness, ennui or mild frustration that the world is not playing out as you hoped. Your Not-Self Theme can emerge as feelings of depression, worrying what else there is to life, feeling let down by humanity, comparison culture… Alternatively, you could go into hyperdrive and try to cram in as many experiences as possible, hedonistically throwing yourself into moving house, switching up jobs, swapping friends, changing partners in a search for 'something' that is already within you. When you feel disappointment appear, look to where it comes from: routine, work, relationships? Explore ways you can be more fluid in those situations to allow you to magnetize more surprise and joy.

You need to be delighted by the magic of life, so focus on feeling open. You will always have interests you are drawn to and, as long as you have the freedom to change when you want to, life will bring you unlimited joy.

REFLECTORS AT WORK

We all spend so much time at work. As a Reflector, your energy levels will reveal whether your job is right for you. Reflect on your work environment and colleagues through your wellbeing. Whatever job you have, you need the freedom to take breaks when required and to know that your feedback is welcomed.

If you dislike your work environment, surround yourself with people who are more supportive, and the same applies to places. This will magnetize your energy and allow the universe to present new opportunities. Be aware that if you are in the wrong environment for a long time, you can become physically unwell through a sick building or draining colleagues.

Reflectors thrive in buzzing atmospheres. You could be CEO of your own brand or manage an HR department. You might also work as a spiritual guide or life coach as you have the intuition to excel. Reflectors have a beautiful gift that allows them to assess the pros and cons of any situation in 360-degree technicolour. In meetings, explain your decisions, thoughts and feelings in a neutral manner. You will often be asked to share your wisdom and insights but you need to find space in a community that sees your special qualities, whether that is online or IRL.

Reflectors are not on this planet to conform, but sometimes you slip into disappointment because you do not fit into regular society's boxes. Never become the person you *think* you should be to fit into a workplace. Instead, move to where you can be your most authentic self. Conditioning makes us believe consistency, particularly in work, is the best way to be, but monotony can lead to the emergence of your Not-Self Theme of disappointment. When the job you once loved feels mundane, you can feel disheartened with your entire life but remember you can be successful even when you are not constantly working and you can make an impact while taking your time.

Some days you might be a powerhouse in the office, and others see you concentrate on contemplative research. Neither are 'better' ways to be; for Reflectors, it is all in the mix.

REFLECTORS AND PEOPLE

To create authentic relationships with friends or in romance, you need to prioritize being kind to yourself. You are crucial to your community and your people will love and support you in more ways than you could ever imagine. If you have not yet found your tribe, or if you feel left out, lean into self-acceptance. When you truly accept yourself, it will allow others to see the true you.

Reflectors mirror all of humanity and have the rare skill to understand people for who they really are. Your aura can quickly sample the energy of a group and work out whether they are your people. If they're not, move on. Allow yourself the power to admit that not liking a vibe is enough reason to leave. If you do end up mirroring another's misdemeanours, remember that it is nothing to do with you. It is simply your energy mirroring theirs and you can clear it out whenever you choose.

Be aware that unaligned Reflectors can slip into passive roles and co-dependency, so do not let others take the lead in life choices or relationships. Build your resilience and independence by spending time alone and socializing with a wide variety of types. Likewise, this will help you avoid simply reflecting the qualities of your partner and allowing you to set boundaries around your own energy. If you have a Reflector friend, let them explore without boundaries and go at their own pace so they can share their wonder and insights with the world.

Famous reflectors

* Dusty Springfield
* H.G. Wells
* Lenny Henry
* Margaret Attwood
* Michael Jackson
* Sandra Bullock
* Uri Geller

Checklist of needs for reflectors

* *Ask yourself who you are going to be every morning when you wake up.*
* *Cultivate self-love by repeating an affirmation in the mirror each morning.*
* *Consider whether you are spending time in the right environment each day at work and in your downtime.*
* *Make space to be with the people who support you and allow you to be your most authentic self.*

- *Create a den or snug in your home where you can be alone to rest and recharge.*
- *Check in to remind yourself that the energies that you take in are not yours, nor do they define you.*
- *Devise a bedtime ritual to clear out the energies you have picked up from the day.*

Crystal kit for reflectors

- Moonstone plugs you straight into the power of the moon.
- Labradorite works as an energetic shield that also amplifies your intuition.
- Calcite is a clarifying stone that will purify any surrounding energies and clear negativity.

Essential oils for reflectors

- Cypress, jasmine, vanilla and frankincense.

Affirmations for reflectors

- I allow space in my life to rest, recharge and clear energy that I've gathered from those around me.
- I am a wise and valued member of my community and I am supported by a loving circle of true friends.
- I am limitless in the abundance, wonder and opportunities that the universe will bring to me.

STRATEGY

STRATEGY

My Strategy is

_____

Each Strategy is intrinsically linked to a Type, so you will have already learnt which Strategy you should be bringing into your life, but it bears repeating. Living your Strategy is one of the most accessible elements of Human Design, yet the results can bring life-changing alignment into every interaction and relationship. Later in this book, when we explore the deeper-dive elements of Human Design, you will see that while fascinating and insightful, those learnings are far less applicable for your day-to-day life. If you want to know how to make things happen and to live most authentically, following your Strategy is how to do it. When you follow your Strategy, opportunities will flow to you and – bonus – you will be able to get what you want with the least amount of effort. The universe does not want you to labour for your goals, but not living in alignment to your Strategy will make getting what you want incredibly tough. Or when you do reach your goal, it is not what you hoped and dreamed it would be...

Have you ever tried to make something happen in your life and turned to self-help books for advice? If you have found they have not worked for you, here is why: so often those suggestions will follow a prescriptive, one-size-fits-all method for smashing your career goals, thriving in relationships or dealing with circumstantial change. They often lead with concepts based around taking charge, chasing change and pushing for what you want. While those methods work for some people, they have not been written for *you*. Your specific Type, your Strategy and your Authority have already been formed into a guide inside you – your personalized self-help manual – which will help you find the path leading to the perfect life for *you*, and which you can follow with minimal effort.

In Human Design, your Strategy will show you how to open yourself up to receive the most wonderful opportunities. Your Strategy has been tailored to your corresponding Type processes information, makes decisions and uses your unique energy. Your Strategy is designed to harmonize with your own capabilities, tendencies and the dynamics already within you. Strategy is the practical reminder of how to deal with any challenge or question that comes your way. When you start to build on your unique gifts with your Strategy at the forefront, you will bring more happiness and success into every area of your life and start living life to your fullest potential.

WAIT TO RESPOND

WHO? Generators and Manifesting Generators

Every action you take needs a signal, an external prompt, before you can launch into any activity. All your energy needs to be directed at the opportunities that will make the most of your dynamism, and that means waiting to respond and *not* initiating something yourself. If that makes you feel twitchy, remember that you have a natural magnetism that will always ensure the right things flow to you. Your part of the deal is to make sure you are aware and paying attention to those prompts and that you are noticing when your gut responds with that warm, expansive feeling.

Waiting to respond will give you valuable time to direct your energy towards people and projects that vibrate with your most authentic self. When a chance presents itself, notice how your gut feels in the moment, then see if you can imagine acting on that opportunity. How would your gut feel if you were living in that new situation? Does it still feel right? Your energy is designed to flow where your gut feels it should be utilized, so avoid getting your brain involved to weigh up the options or asking others for their opinions.

Living your Strategy means your energy does not get wasted (while you have copious amounts of energy, it still shouldn't be squandered) and you can direct your gifts to those people and projects where your input will be welcomed. If you do not, you could slip into your Not-Self Theme of frustration or anger and head towards burnout. When you are attuned to your inner gifts, listening to your gut and taking time to wait to respond you will ensure that you are always making the right decision for you.

TO INFORM

WHO? Manifestors

Communication is key if your Strategy is to inform. For every thought and potential deed that crosses your mind, you need to tell everyone what you are thinking, from where you are going for lunch through to moving to a new country. That sounds over the top. You might feel it is unnecessary to communicate so intensely, but informing will smooth the way for every relationship and allow an array of sparkling opportunities to flow to you. Do not wait for the 'right' moment. When you are informing, be clear that you are not seeking approval, you are just making sure everyone is aware of your actions, before you act. Sometimes it helps to write a list of everyone affected by your plans and to deliver your intentions with empathy. This will allow your plans to come to life with minimum resistance and ensure others will understand and appreciate your motives.

No one knows exactly what your intentions are, but speaking them out loud will help bring them into existence *and* allow you to be noticed and recognized for your talents and skills. The more you are acknowledged, the more at peace you will feel bringing your urges into the world. Manifestors have a deep need to feel supported and that will come by living your Strategy. We have been conditioned to keep our mouths shut and speak only when we are spoken to, so sharing can feel scary to begin with. It could also lead to awkward questions and potential criticism, but being open with your plans and thoughts will allow the universe to magnetize you. This way the right people will come on board and support your visions as it will be clear you are sharing with authenticity.

WAIT FOR THE INVITATION

WHO? Projectors

In a world geared towards go-getting success stories, it can feel agonizing to wait. However, waiting is not a passive act and will ensure any opportunity is perfectly aligned with your purpose. Projectors have incredible wisdom to offer, but you must only share when invited to do so. Unsolicited advice is never welcome and can leave people feeling insecure or negatively towards you, while you will end up bitter (your Not-Self Theme) if your advice is ignored. But once you have an invitation? Go for it! Sharing with those who appreciate your insights will garner recognition and replenish your energies.

Waiting for an invitation does not necessarily mean doing nothing. You need active awareness of your feelings and opportunities. Looking for a new job? Invite old colleagues for lunch, update your LinkedIn page, compile a covering letter that lists your skills or send your CV to your dream companies (then wait for an invitation to interview; if it is meant to be, it will come). If you are self-employed, build a website, put flyers through doors or create a social media presence for your brand.

Outside work, discuss your dreams with your friends and family or build a vision board for how you would like your life to look. Spend time reminding yourself about all the reasons you are so special. For the universe to bring you the right invitations, you need to own your gifts and be confident about your self-worth and skills. Crucially, you need to make sure your availability is clearly signposted. The comments, emails and calls that will flow to you are all invitations that you can respond to. Keep an eye out for hints from people wanting your advice, but who are too shy to ask, as they can be invitations too.

WAIT A LUNAR CYCLE

WHO? Reflectors

While Projectors might feel frustration while waiting for an invitation, Reflectors need to pause for a nail-biting 28 days to reach clarity on the big decisions in life. However, the more you attune to your individual Human Design and start living your Strategy, the easier things will feel. You do not need to wait a month on insignificant decisions, but waiting with awareness will make everything easier. You will be attuned to the natural rhythms that help you thrive and you will start to notice that everything that is right for you arrives with ease, rather than feeling hard or needing to be chased or pushed. When you are living your Strategy, everything flows more smoothly.

If anything in your life grates, ask yourself whether you took a full lunar cycle to come to your conclusion, or whether you were influenced by the thoughts of others on what you *should* do. Because your energies are so influenced by the moon, you need to experience every element of the 28-day lunar cycle – and notice your thoughts and feelings at every stage – before making big decisions. Being around people who appreciate you and recognize your gifts is also key to help you live your Strategy and help you find opportunities in abundance. Be aware that your reflective energies can sometimes mirror those around you, so waiting 28 days will ensure you can understand if what you feel you are being offered is something truly meant for you, or it is for someone close to you. If you notice the same gift returning, or the same feelings throughout the month, the universe will really be directing the opportunity straight to you.

WHAT NEXT?

The next level of living your Human Design is incorporating your Strategy with your Authority (see page 129), If your Strategy advises you how to live your life, checking in with your internal Authority gives an extra layer of validation and ensures you have the energy needed to deal with any situation.

Learning about your own Human Design will show that your Authority is completely unique to you; you will discover exactly how to decipher the way that your inner guidance speaks to you.

Whether you should follow your gut feeling or listen to your intuition depends on your Authority, but mixing the knowledge of the right Strategy for your Type with the inner guidance from your Authority will remove any doubts over decisions and allow you to have complete confidence that you always make the right choice. It is a navigation system unique to you, which will help you overcome conditioning from what society says you *should* do and will help you rise above the unwanted opinions of others.

Combining the guidance of your Strategy and Authority is particularly useful when you come to a point of change in your life. To attune into how to trust your inner navigator, start practising with smaller decisions in your life, such as where to go for lunch or whether to turn left or right on a Sunday stroll. Noticing how your Inner Authority reacts when it is decision time will build your confidence when it comes to bigger choices.

You could also spend time going over past decisions that didn't pan out the way you wanted them to. Consider whether you were living according to your Strategy at the time and then go back and imagine the scenario again, listening to what your Authority would have guided you to do. Can you see if there would have been a different outcome? Even when you appreciate that something was a 'mistake,' the knowledge you have now will certainly help you reach a higher level of understanding and will allow you to trust your inner guidance the next time an opportunity arises.

Likewise, spending time being more mindful will help you tune into your body's messages. Whenever you can tune into your Inner Authority, you will notice its power. Whether you carve out moments to meditate or spend time journalling at the end of the day, any type of mindfulness is powerful as it will bring your awareness of your own body to you, which is key to living your Human Design. Although adhering to your Strategy is one of the easiest ways to get involved with your own Human Design, knowing that you are living your most authentic self is a lifelong process. You will find that you slip away from your path at times, but by returning to honour your Type, listening to your Authority and following your Strategy, you will live with complete authenticity and perfect ease.

AUTHORITY

AUTHORITY

One of the key principles of Human Design is to relinquish using your brain to make decisions. Instead, living your Human Design relies on you listening to your body, guided by your unique Authority, to make the most important decisions in your life.

Our bodies have been created with a higher level of emotional intelligence that our minds do not possess. Neuroscience has shown that our minds are comprised of the logical (left side) and emotional (right side) and they process information, keep us safe and store memories. In fact, they're very good at those jobs, but using your mind to *decide* complicates matters and makes our lives too confusing. Ever suffered decision fatigue? Human Design believes our brains aren't meant to make key decisions. The way a brain is formed in two distinct halves, so how are you ever going to work out which is the 'right' side and 'right' answer?

Throughout the progress of civilization, we have developed a mindset of making practical, logical decisions which does not allow feelings or intuition to have any impact on our plans. When we do allow these elements to creep in, we are often ridiculed. Yet over-thinking is leading to an anxiety epidemic where self-doubt, fear and comparison culture blight our days. As we move into the Age of Aquarius (see page 5), humanity will evolve away from those structures. Tapping into the higher belief that you are an energetic being and should use energy to guide you will help you reach a position of authenticity, where decision-making comes freely. This will come from listening to your Authority.

Think back to when you had to make a decision that changed the direction of your life. Did you struggle? You weighed up all the options, made lists of pros and cons and asked others for their opinions. You second-guessed the outcome (no-one on earth can ever wholly predict what the real results will be or what will happen in the future). You have been conditioned to use so many other tools in the decision-making process, including looking at media, listening to society's rules, considering financial implications, succumbing to peer pressure... You are likely to have become so far removed from living authentically and doing what *felt* right that even when you made that decision and acted on it, it still might not be right for your life. Worrying does not help (instead it triggers anxiety and stress) and we blame so many of the mistakes in our lives on 'wrong' decisions, which moves us into anguish and Not-Self Theme feelings.

How much time have you wasted being caught up in indecision? Imagine never having to labour over a decision again. While your logical mind cannot always be trusted to make the most authentic decisions for you, your unique Authority can. Your Authority is coded into your genes 88 days before birth and it will *always* make the right choice for you. By building your connection to your own inner decision-maker, you can have absolute confidence that decisions guided by your Authority will be reliable, tailor-made for you and aligned to your future path. It is a win-win situation.

It will take time to tune into your Authority and leave your mind-led decision-making behind. It is a journey, but now is a great time to start. Begin by gently releasing your mind from making smaller designs to fine-tune your connection to your Authority. Listen to the messages you receive from your body and start using your Authority for making everyday choices. Each Authority will deliver messages in a different manner and, at the beginning, you might not be ready or able to act on your Authority. However, even just acknowledging the message will help you build confidence through small decisions. Start to note down when and how you receive your Authority's messages and its advice (even if you cannot or do not act on it right away). Make a record in a journal or the notes app in your phone every time you feel its influence and jot down the circumstances, too.

After a few weeks, look back at these records to see credible evidence of your Authority's direction. These evidence-based notes will allow you to build up trust in your Authority's absolute accuracy. As you realize that trusting your Authority *does* work, you will soon be able to lean into its truth on the bigger decisions too, freeing up your mind and taking the aligned path. The more time you spend listening, the more you will strengthen your communication with the entire universe and get into an easier flow of life. Although do not panic if you have moments when you slip back into your conditioned life, rewind to mind-led decision-making or end up living your Not-Self Theme. These are all reminders that will prompt you back into alignment, by the very act of noticing them. Going at your own pace will help you reach new levels of clarity and acting on your Authority will change your life. You will feel confident and have clarity that every decision your body makes will lead you on the right path. It is a blissful state to exist in.

Before we explore the eight Authorities, look back at your Chart to note your own Authority. Each of the Authorities comes directly from a source inside us. Some correspond with a specific chakra centre, while others use a mix of energies within you and from outside. Others, such as Lunar Authority, take their entire guidance from outside. Read the section relevant to your specific Human Design Authority to unlock an enlightened way to make decisions in work, love and life.

My Authority is

_____

EMOTIONAL AUTHORITY

TYPE: Generator, Manifesting Generator, Manifestor, Projector
YOUR TRUTH COMES FROM: The solar plexus centre
ASK YOURSELF: Does this decision make me happy?
TIME FRAME FOR DECISION MAKING: 1 day-1 week

Those with Emotional Authority encounter emotional waves that scoop you up into a high that sees you skipping through your days, but then drop you into a low that leaves you feeling like you got out of bed the wrong side (if you managed to get out of bed at all, that is). Around 50 per cent of the population is led by Emotional Authority, so if you have ever been perplexed by how deeply you experience your emotions or wondered 'Why am I feeling like this?', remember you are not alone. Half the world is experiencing a completely random emotional wave right now.

Although if you are reading this and thinking you are *not* led by your emotions, yet your Human Design says you have Emotional Authority, consider your conditioning. Society often teaches us to have a stiff upper lip and hide our emotions. Showing too much of ourselves can lead us to be labelled as dramatic and giving in to your feelings could make you vulnerable. In every stage of our Human Design journey, it is necessary to decondition ourselves. Now is the time to unpick elements of your life, going back to childhood, and decipher how you have become so removed from your emotions. Were you encouraged to hide your emotions, scolded for being 'too much' or told that people do not want to hear about your feelings? These could all lead you to repress the emotions that are in you and make you feel that you are not attached to your feelings.

Emotional Authority guides you from your solar plexus centre, which focuses on emotions and spiritual and social awareness. Your emotions affect everyone around you – and far beyond – depending on the strength of your emotional waves. Using Emotional Authority as your inner decision-maker requires you to understand your emotional waves and it is crucial you only make important decisions when you have reached an emotionally neutral place.

Arriving at an emotionally neutral place is essential for decision-making because your moods are so impactful on your life. A good mood can frame a dull opportunity as having more benefits than are actually there, while a low mood will stop you getting excited about something potentially brilliant. Sometimes you might be so caught up in your feelings that you just want to move on from decision-making, so you make *any* choice, but you will certainly end up regretting a decision you let your mind make in haste. Relying on brain-led decisions can also lead you to doubt yourself because of 'wrong' choices you made when your wave was high or low, but by listening to your Authority you can remove that doubt.

To start becoming aware of your emotional waves, could you decipher where you are right now? Note it down in a journal, diary or calendar app. Check in several times a day, as well as over the coming weeks. Start keeping a record of your feelings to know what waves might be coming and when they may arrive. The more you understand your waves, the more you can identify when you will be emotionally neutral to allow you to make your best decisions.

Depending on where you are on your wave, and the question in hand, always try to sleep on a decision to reset your energy. Get used to telling people that you will get back to them, or that you need to sleep on it. If you need longer than a night, that is fine too. Everyone takes different amounts of time to come to neutral. Wait. You should never worry that people will have moved on before you have made your decision. If they have, it was not an aligned opportunity for you *anyway*. While you are waiting for clarity, you will notice they probably come back to check in on your decision because everyone wants your unique energy in their life. You may also notice that more people will start to support you and respect your decisions when you share your thoughts after taking your time.

Processing the realization of just how impactful your emotions are on your entire life can feel intense but knowing how you operate will ultimately help you. You will realize that low moments are often a temporary feeling (although if you suffer from persistent depression, do see a medical professional) and when you have the skills to understand your own emotional intelligence, you will see how emotions can be a gift to help you navigate your life. Each emotion was given to you for a reason and your waves can teach you resilience, compassion, wisdom and empathy. When you live your Human Design, you will be able to navigate your waves with calm and acceptance, instead of feeling you *are* the emotion or over-analyzing the places you have been and the people you have spent time with. Tell your friends and family when you are in a low mood due to your waves and they will know to support you or give your space. You may find you move into a guidance role, where you can share your emotional experience to support others.

Likewise, the more you understand your emotional waves are simply energy, you will be able to move on from the conditioned thinking that down moods are 'bad' and happy is 'good'. Labelling your emotions can make you feel guilty or resistant to what you are experiencing, whereas accepting the feelings is a far better way to manage the waves. If you experience intense waves, that impact your daily life, and are not transient, do seek professional medical advice from a doctor. Some Human Design followers may have considered that an emotional wave stems from bipolar disorder or that you suffer from depression. Once you are sure there isn't an underlying medical reason, be aware that you are not the emotion. When you are on a high wave, celebrate by hanging out with friends, dancing or practising gratitude and when you are on a low, cry it out, watch the weepy movies and listen to the saddest songs. Feel the feels. But know that you will always move on. Although if the emotional waves are impacting your life, and are not transient, do seek professional advice from a doctor. If you can, remove yourself from the emotion and see if you can find a lesson to take from the situation. What can you learn from this perspective? Remember that everything will pass. Your emotions should not define you and, annoyingly, *thinking* about the emotion will prolong the time you experience it. although if you suffer from persistent depression, do see a medical professional)

Now you know more about how your body and energies operate, how does that translate to making decisions with Emotional Authority? Whatever opportunity has come to you, make sure you are emotionally in neutral, in a calm space between your waves. Walking barefoot on grass can ground you and release spent emotions. Similarly, it might help to meditate or move into a quiet place where you can imagine yourself in the situation, then tune into your solar plexus chakra, in your belly. Notice what you are feeling. Even though you are imagining the situation and not living in it, with Emotional Authority your body cannot tell the difference. Your Authority will communicate whether the outcome is aligned for you by making you feel happy, or not. By tuning into your body on smaller decisions you will notice the feelings that arrive with aligned choices. You might feel expansion, warm joy or happiness for positive choices. In contrast you might feel smaller, a shrinking sensation, deflation, exhaustion, a knot in your stomach or a contraction for decisions you need to say 'no' to. If you feel nothing or a slightly 'meh' feeling, that is still a 'no'... for now. Do not waste your energy on situations that do not completely light you up and make you joyful. Things might change, so if you cannot clarify your Authority's message, wait until you are back in neutral and check in another day.

One way you might be confused around a decision is through feeling fear. Fear is not necessarily a 'no' because there is still energy behind it. A definite 'no' will leave you feeling those draining, negative sensations, but fear could still be a 'yes'. If you are not sure, give yourself more time to ascertain whether the decision will make you happy and ensure that you are not analyzing the thoughts in your brain and are truly listening to clarity from within your body.

AFFIRMATION: My emotions do not define me, but trusting my body will lead to greater happiness in my life.

SACRAL AUTHORITY

TYPE: Generator, Manifesting Generator
YOUR TRUTH COMES FROM: The sacral centre
ASK YOURSELF: Do I want this?
TIME FRAME FOR DECISION MAKING: Immediately

You might have been told to 'use your head' your entire life, but if you have Sacral Authority, 'follow your gut' is better advice for you. You have been designed to make important decisions by listening to your gut reaction, which will tell you immediately whether it is a chance to take, based on your wants. Your Authority stems from your sacral centre – the origin of life force, creativity and sexuality – and you will experience a rush of visceral excitement when it is a decision worthy of a 'yes' from you. As Generators or Manifesting Generators, your strategy is to wait to respond and your Authority goes hand in hand with this. Do not initiate. Instead, wait for opportunities to come to you. When they do, remove your mind from the decision-making process and let your Authority decide through an immediate bodily reaction, which will guide you to the perfect response. Avoid asking 'are you sure?' as this leads back into mind-led thinking and away from trusting your Authority.

Think back to a moment you made a decision that you later regretted and consider *how* you made *that* choice. Compare this to a time when you made a decision that you are still thrilled with. *How* did you reach *that* outcome? Study the processes to note any differences. Did you spend ages deliberating? Did you do the 'right' thing according to societal conditioning and not what your instincts told you? Were you swayed by the advice of others or felt an obligation? Your unique energy means you should be spontaneous. No-one knows what you need better than you. Your Authority does not know *why* it wants what it does, but when you are tuned into listening to your body, trust that the response will *always* lead to an opportunity that is true and right for your path.

By tuning into your Authority, know that your Human Design will give you a deep-rooted and immediate bodily response when you become excited by something you want. Do not second guess yourself or get caught up in mind-led thinking, just listen to your body and note its reaction in the moment. Remember, there is a difference between your *responses*, which are the calm, measured replies to an invitation, compared to your *reactions*, which are the knee-jerk, instant reflexes.

Handing your decision-making over to your Authority is a gradual process. Start tracking your reactions to small, low-stakes choices before you come to any big, serious decisions. If you have Sacral Authority, you are a 'yes' or 'no' person. You will steer away from grey areas or non-committal maybes. While those with Emotional Authority can imagine situations and judge their body's reaction to something in their mind, those with Sacral Authority need a physical stimulus. Tune in to how you react to actual situations that need an answer, whether that is reading an email or reaching a fork in a road. Listen carefully as your sacral centre's response will fade quickly, but know that if you want it, go for it. Even if it is not logical or practical, the universe will work out how to make the next steps happen. Trust that your gut knows it is the right route for you.

When it comes to honing your trust in your Authority, get granular. Never ask open-ended questions. 'What shall we do this weekend?' is harder for your Authority to answer than 'Shall we go to the cinema or the theatre?' Cutting down your decisions to one choice at a time makes it easier for your gut and therefore simpler for you to trust in each choice your Authority makes.

Your gut does not know 'maybe' or what will happen next (but neither does your brain, remember), so shelve any fear of the future. Your Authority will always give the purest response to situations with a simple 'yes' or 'no', depending on whether it is an outcome it wants *and* whether you have the energy required to make the project come to life.

When something is aligned to you, your sacral centre might give you a feeling of being drawn to it. 'Yes' might feel like a pull of desire, you might say 'Oooh!' or simply cry 'Yes!' You might get a shot of energy or a burst of warmth. In contrast, unaligned options might feel like an internal sigh, your shoulders may slump, or your eyes could roll. You could feel exhausted or your gut may tighten. You might even say 'Nah!' out loud. Society has conditioned us to believe impulsive decisions are irresponsible, but for you spontaneity is the only way to live. Do not be afraid to trust yourself.

If you have no response or feel 'meh' to something, it is still a 'no'. Your Authority only knows what it wants right now, so the same choice might elicit a completely different answer another day. But you need to listen to your gut and do what your body tells you in that moment. Be aware that a contraction in your gut with energy attached, as opposed to a contraction with exhaustion, might be a 'yes' masked by fear. You might need to dig deeper for further information on the opportunity and return to the question at a later date for clarification. If you still feel hesitant, consider if your conditioning is opposing your Authority's choice or if you are allowing your mind to override your gut's decision.

If you know you have a big decision to make, try to ground yourself. Open your throat chakra (by singing, chanting or speaking out loud) or do a check of your five senses to attune yourself to your body, which will allow you to become totally receptive to your Authority's decision. It will always be the right one to make.

AFFIRMATION: I trust my body to always make decisions that are aligned to the best future for me.

SPLENIC AUTHORITY

TYPE: Projector or Manifestor
YOUR TRUTH COMES FROM: The splenic centre
ASK YOURSELF: Does this feel right?
TIME FRAME FOR DECISION MAKING: Immediately

As the home of your sixth sense and instincts, Splenic Authority means important decisions are directed by your intuition. In our bodies, the splenic centre creates energy around physical safety. It is where fear comes from and a healthy approach to fear is necessary to keep us away from danger. If you have ever felt anxious when ignoring your instincts, you will understand that building trust in your intuition will allow you to listen to your Authority, so you can live in alignment with your Human Design.

With every choice, Splenic Authority asks you to tune into your immediate reactions. Your emotional and sacral centres are undefined and you can make an instant decision. You do not need time to reach clarity as you are blessed with consistent energy, but although it is fast, your Authority delivers soft, quiet communications that are delivered only once. Tuning into your inner guidance is necessary to ensure you do not miss a message.

As your big decisions are designed to be spontaneous and led by your sixth sense, your truth will come at the exact time of decision. If you miss the signal, hold off from a response until your Authority is audible again. At that point, know that it is *you* who holds the best guidance for your journey ahead. Believing in your intuition will allow you to rise above anxiety and fears attached to decision-making and free you to believe your instincts are telling you the ultimate truth, at all times. If you have ever felt weighed down by imposter syndrome or doubted your worth, you are likely to have dulled your intuition. You do not need to explain your intuition to others unless you want to, but now is the time to bring it back into your life.

Because Splenic Authority delivers its message so subtly, spend time attuning to your body so you do not miss the signal. You could try meditating to see if you are able to quieten the noise in your life and notice the communication. It could be indistinct to begin with, but the more you practice, the clearer and louder it will become. You might feel a stirring sensation or have visions. Splenic Authority originates deep inside your body and may whisper its guidance, rather than shout. You may feel an almost imperceptible lightening – or weighing down – of your load. Things may just feel illogically 'right' or 'wrong' but do not ignore the message, however muted. Splenic Authority is a quiet power that is lightning fast. If you start to consider the decision, it means you have moved into the mind and the moment will have passed, so go back and ask again.

Take physical notes in a journal or on your phone so that you are aware of when and how you get a message. This written record of the power of your intuition will allow you to start trusting your body and relegate the chatter in your mind that constantly debates decisions in your head. If you can do any of this outside, in nature, it will lead to even clearer answers.

The more you ask your spleen questions, the more open your communication channels will become. Start small by checking in on what route to take to work or where to go for lunch. Listen and note the response. You can ask your spleen anything and, once you have a strong connection, you will delight in the realization that your spleen is *always* there to support you. Imagine the freedom of never having to overthink a situation again! If you ever feel you cannot get a proper answer from your spleen, doublecheck whether you are allowing your mind a say in the matter. Overthinking could overwhelm your Authority's instincts as you might have started mulling over a matter after you had the message.

AUTHORITY

As you lean into guidance from your Authority, you might falter and feel Splenic Authority results in irrational and inconsistent decisions. But your spleen is not rational. Splenic Authority is intuitive. Remember, your guidance is unique to you and comes directly from the universe, not through a list of pros or cons. If you have ever had to act on an urge to leave a venue, or go somewhere urgently, you will have been in tune with your splenic instinct. As you are reading this book, I imagine you are open to things that you do not *have* to see to understand, but if you have ignored your inner voice and only believed what you *can* see and understand, you may find the transition harder. Persevere with the shift and it will be more than worth it.

To attune to Splenic Authority, start by bringing your attention to your core and ask a question. Listen hard and note your instinctive response. A clear 'right' or 'wrong' feeling will show you the way, but if there is no obvious response, revisit the question another time. Lack of feeling or a 'meh' response are also negative responses because you need to save your energy for what is truly aligned to you. When you come back to the question, focus on whether it *feels* right. When it does, it is now right for you. Instead, take immediate action and remove any fear of the future. When you are led by your Authority, it will always be the right decision.

AFFIRMATION: I am led to decisions that are right for me by listening to my intuition and instincts.

EGO-PROJECTED AUTHORITY

TYPE: Projector
YOUR TRUTH COMES FROM: The ego/heart centre
ASK YOURSELF: Does this serve me?
TIME FRAME FOR DECISION MAKING: Immediately

Only 1 per cent of the population have Ego-Projected Authority. You have been designed to use your ego centre to guide you towards decisions that truly enhance your life. On your Body Graph your heart is defined and connected to your throat, but because you have so many undefined centres, Not-Self thoughts and feelings can appear throughout your life. When it comes to decision-making, your Authority will advise on whether it is something that will benefit you *and* whether you have the energy to go for it. Remember, Projectors have limited energy supplies, so you should only apply your precious reserves to things that will truly benefit you.

As very small children we are told that saying 'I want' is rude. You may have felt you needed to tone down your desires throughout your entire life, because want is associated with greed. However Human Design does not apply such values to emotions. If you want something, that is simply a sign from the universe to go for it. Your wants can be a way to drive you forward. Of course, some wants can be 'bad' if they mean other people lose out or suffer for you to have your desires, or if you slide into feelings of superiority, but wants *and* needs are ultimately energetically neutral.

With Ego-Projected Authority, you are guided by the heart centre which chimes with self-worth, motivation, value and willpower. These are often linked to outside recognition, so you may sometimes fall victim to self-doubt or feelings of low self-worth. You might have struggled in situations where you think you could have done more, but when you are on an aligned path for your Type, Strategy and Authority know that you absolutely deserve to be selective over the projects you choose. You should share your gifts only with those who truly appreciate you.

When presented with a choice, you should always ask 'What's in it for me?' Your Human Design has one of the only Authorities that takes money into consideration and your unique path connects you to material goods. Particularly in New Age spheres, it can feel crass or selfish to consider cold hard cash but reflect on the phrase 'enlightened selfishness'. Simply put, it is a belief that when something serves you to the highest degree, it can only be beneficial to others, too. Set aside any conditioned thoughts of being selfish, fear of appearing materialistic or not believing wealth and true altruism can go together. If it is due to you, it is your right to have the fame, money or success you want.

Your Authority comes from inside your chest, so start by focusing on where your heart is in your physical body. You might feel a buzz of excitement or expansion when an aligned choice appears. Alternatively, you could notice a tangible sinking or shrinking sensation. Ask how the project could serve you? Will it bring money, influence or expansion that benefits you? Will you be rewarded or compensated in a way you deserve? Is your heart really in it? Tune in and notice how your heart feels with smaller decisions. This will help build up awareness of your Authority when it comes to larger changes. Non-responses or 'meh' feelings are also unaligned – a sense of support in your choice is essential. If you do not have clarity, wait and ask again, as many times as you need until you feel a clear response. If an opportunity will not elevate you, it will be a sacrifice. Always believe that something better will come along (and it will) so do not waste your energy on anything other than opportunities that resonate at your highest alignment. You might find you need to ask a series of difficult questions to get to the truth of an opportunity; doing all you can to gain absolute clarity will help your heart make the right decision.

While you have huge reserves of empathy and are influenced by others, move away from thinking you need to consider their opinions before you make your choice. Instead, ponder whether you have any self-limiting beliefs around your own self or your financial worth. You might find others try to stand in your way but tell them your plans and then remind yourself of your incredible willpower. Build a moodboard of your dream life and think limitlessly about what you want to achieve. It might sound simplistic, but what you want needs to happen.

AFFIRMATION: I deserve all I desire because it is for the greater good of all around me.

EGO-MANIFESTED AUTHORITY

TYPE: Manifestor
YOUR TRUTH COMES FROM: The ego/heart centre
ASK YOURSELF: Does this serve me?
TIME FRAME FOR DECISION MAKING: Immediately

Your Authority aligns with the chakra that is associated with motivation, will-power and feelings of value and self-worth. Your energy has a consistent drive and your heart needs to want something to make any decision worth your while.

Sometimes you might not actually know what you want, but when you hear yourself speak about it, your heart will instantly know whether it is an opportunity that will serve you and benefit you to the highest level. When you have a big decision to make, Ego-Manifested Authority means you just need to open your mouth to listen to your truth. Pointers to the correct decision will flow straight from your heart and show you the right path to take.

Your wants are closely linked to material things, so any project you undertake needs to serve you financially as well as with proper respect for your skillset. You might feel vulgar or vulnerable when asking questions about money, but it is essential you are honoured with significant investment. It is also key that you put aside your conditioning around appearing greedy, overly materialistic or believing you need to steer clear of money talk to avoid confrontation. You absolutely deserve material wealth. If your Authority wants it, it will be aligned to help you on a path that will create the best life for yourself and for others around you.

You are incredibly open to other people's energy and can get caught up in their emotions, so make time to focus on *your* needs and bring 'enlightened selfishness' into your life. This is a belief that when a want serves you to the highest degree, it is never traditionally selfish as it is beneficial to others, too.

When it is time to make a decision, ensure you have gathered enough information about the opportunity, including how it will serve you and any associated benefits. Do not rush to listen to any voices in your head or control the outcome. Instead, if you have Ego-Manifested Authority you need to speak out loud for clarity to come. You can talk to a friend, partner or trusted colleague, the universe or simply yourself. Remove any barriers to speaking out loud that might subconsciously sift out your truth. Speaking out loud is your unique way of getting attuned to the truth. Listening to your words is obviously important, but note your tone and inflection, too. When a decision is the right one, your voice will become clear and confident, or you will hear the excitement and enthusiasm as you talk. It is important to speak in an environment where you feel safe. If the decision is not right for your path, your voice may sound heavy. You will use negative phrases or indifferent language. You may also feel an expansion in your chest for 'yes' decisions or a contraction when it is a 'no'. Sometimes you might not be able to decipher the truth because you feel neutral or indifferent, but understand that those are not the right opportunities for you now. You could check in again at a later date, but expending energy on anything other than what sets your heart fire will drain you. A better opportunity will always come along and you should never settle for something mediocre when brilliance is out there waiting for you.

When it is time to make your decision, it is key to remember that you do not need to consider the opinions of others. If you are speaking out loud to someone, politely let them know that you do not need their input, simply a sounding board. True friends will always understand this and you should discard any worries that being open makes you vulnerable, or that you are offending others by not taking their advice. Your inner truth needs to be heard by you and your Authority alone is the best way to decide the route to take on your path to greatness.

Unlike other Authorities, your Human Design does not take in prompts from the outside world. To bring you to the point of decision, spend time meditating or vision-boarding around what your dream life would be. Put aside any practical constraints and think big! Tell yourself you deserve everything in life and know you have the capacity to make all your dreams come true.

AFFIRMATION: I have the strength and willpower to accomplish whatever I desire.

SELF-PROJECTED AUTHORITY

TYPE: Projector
YOUR TRUTH COMES FROM: The G centre
ASK YOURSELF: Will this bring me closer to my life's purpose?
TIME FRAME FOR DECISION MAKING: Immediately you have spoken out loud

Sometimes also known as the G-Centre Authority, Self-Projected Authority means your intuitive thoughts need to be written down or voiced out loud for you to gain clarity over decision-making. Your G-centre chakra corresponds with your life's direction and purpose. Your unique energy has been designed to flow when you use your voice to release the truth inside you. You may find you sit and mull over decisions for days, weighing up options alone, and while this can help you understand a choice ahead, up to a point, it will not deliver the actual decision. To do this, once you have opened your mouth and can talk freely, you will find the truth in a situation through speech. Speaking out loud will also help to simplify tricky situations that seem complicated in your mind. Voice your feelings to as many different people as possible. If you do not have a trusted friend close by, you can record yourself talking and play it back later. You could also journal your thoughts, then read your words aloud to reach clarity on the path you need to take.

If you are talking to a friend, make sure they know you do not need their approval, input or advice on your decision; they just need to be a sounding board for you to voice your own truth.

Any aligned invitation must bring you joy and excitement, and for you to know it will bring you closer to your life's purpose. Once you speak, you will be able to *hear* whether you have enthusiasm and passion in your voice, as well as from the subconscious choice of words you actually speak.

As a Projector, you have a wonderful gift of seeing the paths others should take, but you sometimes struggle to define your own path and acknowledge your innate brilliance. You may move from feeling that you speak too much and take up too much space to a fear of public speaking and not wanting to be the centre of attention. While you are conflicted, the world can see your unique gifts and the more you speak out loud, the more attuned you will be to your G-centre and can start to truly know yourself. Candid speech, when those who value your worth are listening, will help bring your truth to the fore.

When it is time to make a big decision, and you have considered all the options in your mind, open your mouth and let your honesty flow without editing your words. Consider whether the choice will lead you closer to your life's purpose and keep you heading in the right direction. The passion, excitement and joy for an aligned choice will be clear to hear and you may feel your chest expanding with positivity. Conversely, if your delivery is dull, you feel pushed away from a choice or your words are indifferent, this will be a 'no' for you. You may feel fear creep into your thoughts as you are speaking, but keep talking through any anxieties, letting your truth flow from your G centre. At times you may also notice your Not-Self Theme of bitterness appearing from your undefined centres and starting to influence your feelings, but ignore those notions. Keep talking. At any point in your decision-making, if you *think* you could, you feel you *have to* or you feel sorry for someone, then however much you think it is a 'yes', it is a not an aligned opportunity for you right now.

On the days you have a big decision to make, try to warm your voice up and open your energy centre by talking about something neutral, such as a book you are reading or by describing your last meal. Recording yourself will help you capture brilliant ideas, particularly when it comes to work, and anytime you feel anxiety clouding your thoughts, find a mantra to say out loud to re-centre you. In fact, starting every day by saying your intentions out loud and making a gratitude list before bed (and reading it out loud) will be beneficial to living your Human Design.

You may be struggling to define your life's purpose, feeling lost or that you are too dependent on others. Talking to yourself, singing in the shower or the car or reading books out loud will all help your throat chakra open, and allow you to connect with your Authority. Likewise, journalling and free writing (and then reading your words out loud) will also help strengthen the energetic bond. It would be particularly useful to you to think back to childhood. Remember the hobbies you loved and the way you expressed yourself, before conditioning and adulting got in the way. This can also lead you to reconnect with your future purpose and path ahead.

AFFIRMATION: I always reach the best truth for me when I voice my inner intuition out loud.

MENTAL/ENVIRONMENTAL AUTHORITY

TYPE: Projector
YOUR TRUTH COMES FROM: The whole body
ASK YOURSELF: Does this decision feel right?
TIME FRAME FOR DECISION MAKING: Once you have processed the options

Less than 1 per cent of the population have Mental/Environmental Authority. When you consider how many people on the planet there are, that is a significant number, but you are still a rare gem. Some Charts may state your Inner Authority as 'none' and you are the exception to one of Human Design's key principles. Human Design focuses on moving away from mind-led thinking, but if you have Mental Authority, it is essential to consider all the options when it comes to making a big decision... and use your mind to do so! However, you then need to physically move into an array of environments to reach clarity, which you will feel in your whole body.

Walking and talking with a trusted friend will be a great way to sound out your thoughts, but make sure your companion knows that you do not need advice. Keep your boundaries in place, so you are not swayed by others' opinions in your decision-making process. True friends will respect your need for space. You are vulnerable to other people's energy, which can overwhelm you with their fears and emotions, but being in places that fill you up, that feel wholesome and nourishing for you, will help you immensely. Spend as much time as you can in nature.

All the definition in your Body Graph is above the throat, which means you have extreme empathy and feel the world around you deeply. Your mind, also known as ajna or awareness, takes control of your decision-making. But even though your mind is in charge of making decisions, note that you have a mind to think, process and plan with *and* an intuitive mind that is full of sparkling energy. Projectors have a unique gift for developing new processes around the way we live our lives. Your insights and uncommon perspectives will improve the world and it is important to understand that your brain is truly brilliant, but it cannot make decisions for you. When you have Mental Authority, your thinking mind will always try to solve a problem, but your decision-making mind goes deeper. It does not need a list of pros and cons, it just *knows*. When you are heading for an aligned decision, your intuition will always give you a feeling that it is the right thing to do, but which you cannot explain.

When you have a big decision, deliberate and cogitate as much as you can. Make those lists, analyze the spreadsheets and doublecheck the fine print. Afterwards, head to a place you love (to fulfil the Environmental part of your Authority) and notice the feelings that flow to you. Whether you are in a cozy coffee shop, a friend's house, the local park, a beach or your own garden, this special place will shed light on the right direction. If you need more clarity, talking about your decision with friends, ideally in this special place, will help you hear your truth. Your aura needs to connect with others and as you speak, listen to your words. If you repeat the same things or say something consistently, you will recognize the right path for you.

While some Authorities come to a decision immediately, if you decide something instantly, it will only allow a tiny fraction of yourself to get involved. Instead, wait for your whole being to reach clarity and keep weighing up the information. When you feel that you have done all the research possible, this will lighten your mind and allow the environment to step in with the truth. You will feel an aligned decision in the core of your body. If it is an aligned choice, you may notice a lightness, or you might experience a heavier feeling for unaligned choices. If you are left emotionless or just feel okay about a decision, it is a 'no' for now. Projectors have less energy than other Types and so you need to protect the energy you do have by avoiding situations that are not completely right for you. Before you reach a big decision, practise tuning into your mind centre and familiarizing yourself with your special environments so you can understand what a 'yes' decision feels like for you. When you are done with your decision, try leaving an offering in that place, such as flowers, a candle or a crystal, as a thank you to the universe.

As you practise tuning into your Authority, it is worth remembering that making decisions in this considered manner does not make you indecisive, nor are irrational decisions less valid. Work out which processes help you the most, whether it is journalling, making lists, creating spreadsheets or mind-mapping. You can sometimes fall prey to over-analyzing things, but when you are done with your research, move on by changing your environment or meditating to release the mental pressure. You are so in tune to the energies of different places, when you do not feel at ease in any space, it is important for you to move on immediately.

AFFIRMATION: I know my mind and intuition will always show me the right decision and I allow my chosen environments to create a safe space for me.

LUNAR AUTHORITY

TYPE: Reflector
YOUR TRUTH COMES FROM: The whole body
ASK YOURSELF: Does this decision feel right?
TIME FRAME FOR DECISION-MAKING: After a lunar cycle

Only Reflectors will have Lunar Authority, although some Charts may list your Inner Authority as None. For big decisions you need to wait 28 days for clarity, which is aligned with your Strategy. As a Reflector, you will be getting used to how your feelings traverse the full lunar cycle and the wonderful opportunities you have by becoming a different person every day.

Your Body Graph will show that your Centres are all undefined, which means you take on the energy of the people around you and the environments you are in, as well as that of the moon. If you are with a spontaneous decision-maker, you might feel that you are able to make an immediate decision that would reflect who you were with, where you were at that moment and the position of the moon, rather than waiting for true clarity. While you can share the energy of those you spend time with, you must take care not to take on their qualities. That is why you need the full lunar cycle to ensure that temporal energy does not influence your decisions. Talking to a trusted friend could help you articulate your thoughts on a decision, but only discuss your feelings with those who will listen rather than offer advice. Find a mantra that will help you reiterate your confidence in your own decisions and spend time building trust in yourself to help yourself move away from being influenced by others.

As you pivot through the moon's transits, you might feel that you are inconsistent, but because the moon makes her journey through your gates in the same pattern each month, you are actually *very* consistent! Your energy is most affected by the moon and as it shifts into your Gates, new experiences will illuminate different parts of your Chart, allowing you to feel different things. This means you can go with the flow for small decisions, but what if it is a big deal? Wait until you have completed a full lunar cycle.

Check which moon phase you are in whenever a question crops up and wait until that phase comes round again to share your decision. Skip looking inside yourself for the answers. Your undefined centres mean you need an external source of clarity. During the lunar cycle, journal about who you are each day and how you feel about the decision, but try to remove yourself from making an actual decision. Simply observe your feelings, without pressuring yourself to find an answer. You could get a moon calendar or app so you can easily work out which part of the cycle you are in. If you have periods, you could track your menstrual cycle alongside this, too. Do not be worried about admitting how you feel every day or believing you must hide your sensitivity – your true friends will always support you and you will gain more respect by living authentically.

At some point during the lunar cycle, clarity will land in your lap and you will instinctively know which way to turn. When you have reached an aligned decision, you will feel it across your whole body with a wonderful lightness or expansion, while heaviness or contraction – again, across your entire being – are 'no' verdicts. No clarity or a 'meh' sensation also mean 'no'. If you have gone through the full lunar cycle and you have yet to reach clarity, wait another month. You need to be completely sure of your next move as you are a non-energy being. You cannot share your limited energy with projects that are not aligned for you. Sometimes fear might cloud your decision-making abilities and can hide aligned decisions. As always, take your time and check in again once a further 28 days have passed.

At the start of your Human Design journey, waiting a full lunar cycle can be particularly tough. Life has conditioned us to make decisions ASAP, reply to emails before EOP and act fast, so we do not miss out. However, the universe takes its own sweet time. The universe will reveal the right decision for you at the right moment and you do not have to do anything (in fact you *should not*). Reflectors can sometimes get over-attached to the mood, energy, people or places you are in, which can make everything feel right (it is akin to how those with Emotional Authority can feel falsely positive when they are on the high of an emotional wave), but you must give decisions time for these transient feelings to pass, so you do not get caught up in a distorted sense of security.

It is going to be tricky to surrender to your Authority, but you need to believe that taking your time does not make you indecisive. Likewise, you will not miss out on opportunities by waiting. If the chance or person has moved on, it was not something aligned for you. Do not be afraid to trust yourself. Every morning, try to ground yourself and spend time in nature to set yourself up for the day ahead. Then, when you leave an environment – say, work or a party – establish an energy-clearing ritual to move on from other people's energies. Perhaps you can incorporate a cleansing shower, using an essential oil or working with crystals to help you? Other ideas are listed in the chapter on Authority (see page 99). You could do this before bed. If you can end your day in the moonlight, it will be super-beneficial to tuning into your Lunar Authority, too.

AFFIRMATION: I am unafraid to wait to make my decisions and never allow others to influence my choices.

CENTRES

CENTRES

Now you recognize your personality traits, know the best way for you to make decisions and understand how to navigate your life, learning the principles of your Centres will reveal how your body communicates. Ever wondered why you walk into a room and start chatting to one person while swerving to avoid another? It is simply energy. We all have energy flowing in and out of our Centres, moving to and from other people. The direction of this energy, and how our body processes it, is why we are attracted to or repelled by different people. Do not take it personally. It is just an exchange of energy and depends on the combination of defined and undefined Centres you share – or not – with those who surround you. This energy is the force that drives us, inspires us, sparks relationships, leads our intuition *and* our emotions. It is a lot!

Learning about your individual mix of Centres is important to avoiding negative self-talk and looking after the VIPs in your life. Awareness of your Centres allows you to focus on your strengths and get help when struggling with tasks you are not designed to do alone.

Some Centres have the same names as body parts, but they correspond with internal zones, rather than specific organs. In Human Design, your Centres are similar to the chakra system. Think of your Body Graph as an X-ray of the energy you have available to you and be aware that if you are out of alignment with your Centres, you may find you have physical symptoms in those areas and organs. If you are unwell or experiencing symptoms, always seek immediate advice from a medical professional.

To find your Centres, look at your Body Graph. On the silhouette of your torso, Centres are represented by the nine squares, triangles and diamond shapes. Some are coloured in, while others are colourless. Each Centre equates to the ways you are meant to influence the world *and* the ways you can be influenced, depending on whether your Centres are coloured or colourless. If the shape is coloured, that means the Centre is *defined* and somewhere you share energy. An uncoloured shape is *undefined* and a place you can be influenced by others' energy.

DEFINED

A defined Centre has a Channel that connects it to another Centre. Channels are the lines that run between the shapes on your Body Graph (we will look at them in more detail in Chapter 9). When a Centre is defined, it means you can always access that Centre's energy. Each Centre corresponds with an emotion like confidence or fear and how we express ourselves. The energy in a defined Centre is a consistent part of your aura's frequency and it will remain part of your life forever. Because defined Centres are constant, you can always rely on them to give you the energy you need.

It is key to note that, as with all energy in Human Design, your Centres are neutral. Defined does not mean *good* and your defined Centres do not correspond to something as conventional as a 'strength'. Likewise, undefined Centres certainly are not *bad* or places of 'weakness'. However, when you are living in alignment to your Human Design, you will live your most abundant life through your defined Centres. You will be consistent, confident and leading the way in that area. When you are unaligned with your defined Centres, you might want to hide away, you could feel small or you may withdraw into your Not-Self Theme. Defined Centres are from where you transmit energy, which can influence others around you, but you cannot take in another's energy through a defined Centre.

OPEN

With a completely open Centre, you do not have any defined Channels or Gates (the numbers around the edge of your Centres on your Body Graph). Defined Gates are like energy filters. Without definition, you could be extra sensitive in that area and more at risk of conditioning. However, awareness will help you notice any conditioned 'should' feelings and allow you to move back into listening to your Authority for true guidance and following your Strategy for the most aligned route in your life. Open Centres take in energy and then amplify it. Some undefined or open Centres communicate more forcefully than others – there is a hierarchy of Centres – and this can sometimes confuse even the most positive flow of energy. Remember, open Centres are still not areas of weakness, they just present another way for you to understand life. Open and undefined Centres give you extra experiences, a wider range of wisdom and further opportunities to share your knowledge with the world.

UNDEFINED

If you have an undefined Centre, you will have at least one defined Gate but no defined Channels. Undefined Centres are where you take in energy from people around you, places, the moon's transit and planetary influences. You will experience that energy, then amplify it. Your undefined Centres are where you can be most flexible, open-minded and can also feel the effects of others' energies, opinions and ideas. You can sometimes feel even more deeply than the people around you who have a defined Centre. But remember, while their energy is yours to sample, experience and borrow, it is not yours to keep and that energy does not characterize you.

While you are open to influence, you are still responsible for your actions and having an undefined Centre does not make you another's pawn. Being out of alignment may cause you to mix up the emotions of others with your own and having an undefined Centre can leave you more susceptible to conditioning or feelings of obligation. When you leave the presence of someone with a defined Centre, you might experience a sensation of loss – like you are missing something – but this will pass. You could practise a grounding ritual to bring you back into your own energy.

When your undefined Centres are in alignment, you may experience extreme empathy and heightened wisdom. A wonderful consequence of having undefined Centres is that you might find more enlightenment in these areas, as they will give you unexpected opportunities to expand your understanding and knowledge (compared to defined Centres, which are just doing a job and you may take for granted, due to their continual presence).

The most influential undefined Centres are the heart, solar plexus, identity centre, spleen and ajna (mind or awareness Centre), while the least influential undefined Centres are the throat, sacral centre, root and head. If any of the most influential Centres are undefined on your own Body Graph, be particularly vigilant for feelings of depression, anxiety, stress, tiredness or being stuck, or if you notice your Not-Self Themes appearing. While you can be aligned or unaligned in both your defined and undefined Centres, it is more usual to experience unalignment through your undefined Centres. An off-kilter feeling can lead to your Not-Self Themes, so in each Centre's undefined section, there is an affirmation to help you get back to your best, most-aligned self.

Read the introduction for every Centre and then focus on the section relating to your personal Chart, depending on whether your Centre is defined or undefined. This will give you the most clarity over the themes that will play out in your life.

My defined Centres are

_____

HEAD

This is a pressure Centre, responsible for inspiration, imagination and analysis. It is physically linked to the pineal gland. Your Head Centre is where curiosity comes from, where you find the drive to search for answers and push forward your thinking. Your Head Centre processes your experiences, analyses your doubts and deals with confusion.

DEFINED

Whether it is a concept that fascinates you, you are mulling over past conversations or you are planning the future, you are always thinking. You want to understand *everything*. You can find it hard to switch off and so you need a method to burn off your mental energy. Try writing, debating, reading or playing puzzles; anything that fires up your mind will help you to relax. Some people zone out with reality TV, but your unused mental energy needs more dynamic activities or you can slide into anxiety or depression. You have learned that Human Design is based around moving away from mind-led thinking, as it generates so much anxiety and spirals us into obsessing over things that really do not matter, so allow your Authority to take control of decisions and use your Head Centre for energy only.

When you are in alignment with your Centre you will inspire yourself, and others, with game-changing thinking. As long as you are following your Strategy and Authority, say what you think. Your naturally curious nature could help you solve the world's biggest problems. When you are out of alignment, you may suffer from self-doubt, confusion or anxiety, and you might find yourself pushing others to accept your opinions and ideas. You are not easily swayed by the thoughts of those around you and will often find others waiting to hear your hot take on a topic.

UNDEFINED

When you are around someone with a defined Head Centre, you might find yourself amplifying their anxiety, stress and inner doubts, so be aware when your mind starts spinning or your Not-Self Themes appear. With an undefined Head Centre, you might find yourself returning to think your way through decisions, when your Authority needs to take charge.

When you are in alignment with your undefined Head Centre, you will be open-minded and freely inspired by those around you. You can intuitively understand the ideas of others and are discerning over whose thoughts you allow into your own aura.

Conversely, when you are out of alignment, you might spiral into worrying about unimportant things or feel you have to solve everyone else's problems. You might look for answers from other people or need external inspiration to start a project and will try to keep conversations superficial.

You are susceptible to overwhelm and may feel pressured to always have a response ready. You may feel embarrassed when you do not know all the answers. Instead, reframe your thinking. It is not the answers that excite you, rather it is the journey of discovering the truth. Realizing that you do not know everything can liberate you to explore areas that are worth thinking about. Follow your Strategy and Authority for clues, and when your Head Centre is undefined, revel in the chance to investigate all the world can share with freedom.

AFFIRMATION: I know that the answers will come to me when the time is right.

AJNA

This is an Awareness Centre, which shapes how you form opinions and conceptualize the world. Physically linked to the pituitary gland, your ajna is linked to mental awareness, ideas and theories. In Sanskrit, ajna means 'to command' and while ajna commands the traditional chakra system, in Human Design it processes energy to help us gain perspective.

DEFINED

Your way of thinking is consistent, which helps hone your opinions and influences and inspires others. Your mind is a constant whirr and you may find it hard to relax, so make sure you have tried-and-tested methods that help you unwind. You could spend the rest of your life considering the options, but let your Authority take on big decisions to give you some peace. Be vigilant: if your mind tries to creep into the decision-making process, this means you are heading out of alignment. Do not get caught up in sweating the small stuff or re-playing past conversations. Remember everyone is waiting to hear your opinions.

When you are living in alignment with a defined ajna, you will revel in opportunities for mental stimulation and chances to be creative. Other people's opinions will not worry you and you will be cast as a thought leader with boundless ideas. Although you do not need to act on all of them, share your thoughts so that others can ponder your theories. The ajna fears being misunderstood, so following your Strategy will also ensure you are sharing your ideas only with people who will honour your energy, and at the right time.

UNDEFINED

When you are in alignment, you have the unique opportunity to understand a huge array of concepts and are flexible and open-minded. You know the topics that matter right now and are intuitively guided to people who have solutions. However, this is balanced by worries that you do not know what to do with your life or cling to other people's ideas and repeat their opinions to feel secure. When you are living out of alignment with an undefined ajna, you might feel nervous about sharing your own thoughts due to worries about being judged or that you do not have enough intellectual knowledge. Ignore those worries.

You may feel like you are living apart from humanity at times and are weighed by pressure to be certain… but you are not designed to be certain. Your open mind is built to explore all the possibilities and you do not need to know all the next steps in your life or the projects you are involved in. You have such sharp mental energy, release any preconceived ideas or outdated philosophies and allow yourself to sink into your wonderful gift for deep contemplation.

AFFIRMATION: I rely on my inner guidance to find my own way forward.

THROAT

This is a manifestation Centre, which guides the way you communicate and express yourself. It is the Centre linked to deciphering what you want to contribute to the world and is physically attached to the thyroid. On your Body Graph, your Throat Centre shares your inner world with the outer world through the 11 Channels that flow from it. These Channels take energy and messages from other Centres and broadcasts them to the world.

DEFINED

Some people switch opinions and voices depending on who they are with, but if your Throat Centre is defined, you are bound by consistency and will always stay the same. Your gift is that you know when to speak and when to be silent, plus you can tune into your Authority to guide you on the best ways to use your energy. A defined Throat Centre carries much responsibility. How you communicate depends on which other Centres your

Throat Centre is connected to: your heart focuses on yourself; your ajna communicates the mind's thoughts; and your solar plexus acts on your emotions. A connection to the spleen means you will communicate your instant intuition while your Sacral Centre allows you to act on a gut reaction. When you are living out of alignment you might shrink to fit a situation and are either pushy around others or chase people away. You may slip into thoughts that you do not matter or need to play down your talents. However, when you are living in alignment, your consistent communication is golden and you can smoothly tap into the perfect timing of your Strategy and Authority's guidance.

UNDEFINED

Although you find it easy to advocate for others by giving a voice to those who cannot speak up, you struggle to acknowledge your own self-worth or talk about your skills and goals. This unaligned inconsistency may lead you to think you need to make things happen and end up interrupting, shouting or blurting out just to get noticed. Sometimes you might start talking with no idea where your train of thought will take you, which can lead to awkward moments. Take time to listen to your inner guidance. Your Strategy will ensure you are speaking at the right moments, around the right energies and for aligned reasons, while your Authority will guide you to speak the truth.

By comparison, when you are aligned with an undefined Throat Centre, you are a confident listener, you can speak without fear – and at the right time – and you enjoy expressing your opinions. Know that you never need to make anything happen, even when you are feeling small and insignificant. Your energy will always attract the right people and opportunities, so trust that you *will* get noticed. Never speak to fill a silence. As you are a Generator, Projector or Reflector, wait until you are asked to share and move away from any thoughts that you need to be doing, making, speaking or creating before you are asked.

AFFIRMATIONS: I attract others simply by being my true authentic self.

G OR IDENTITY

This is an Identity Centre, responsible for how you decipher your life's direction, connecting to your higher self and spirituality. Physically associated with the liver and blood, your G or Identity Centre holds the knowledge of the ability to love and be loved.

DEFINED

Your sense of self and identity is consistent and while you intrinsically know who you are, outside conditioning can weaken this belief. You might find you are particularly gifted at helping others find their purpose in life and offer welcome guidance to those questioning humanity. But do not be put off if you are met with resistance at times. Not everyone is going the same way as you. Be aware if you are forcing anyone to go in your direction, or if you feel you are dimming your own light to fit in. When you are in alignment, you are independent, focused on your own mission and have complete strength of conviction through knowing who you are and what you love.

UNDEFINED

Just because your G-Centre is undefined, it does not mean you lack direction and purpose. You are designed to find your route a different way, so pay close attention to your Strategy and Authority for signposts. You may feel like you *have* to search for your identity, direction or love and fall into inconsistency, so note these signs as warnings of your Not-Self Themes appearing. You will never need to search. At times you might yearn to find a soul mate and discover your purpose, but know that you have so many golden opportunities ahead of you.

Your undefined G-Centre allows your energy to be flexible, which means you can adapt to many different situations. You can clearly see other people's purpose and direction, which makes you an excellent advice giver. You love having many interests and can blend into a variety of environments.

When you are unaligned, you may feel you need others to show you your true self. This means you can be needy and cling onto negative people and situations, just to have direction. However you are feeling, know that you are not lost or and that you are loved. You will find your path and discover your true self if you are spending time in the right places, with the right people – and if a place does not feel right, get out of there immediately.

AFFIRMATIONS: There are infinite ways to discover my purpose.

EGO OR HEART

This is a motor energy Centre, which is physically linked to the digestive system and heart. The heart represents our sense of power and place in the world – exactly our ego – and the Ego Centre guides our drive, conviction, self-worth and material desires. When someone is described as having a 'big ego', it is always delivered negatively. However, believing you are inferior to others is similarly damaging as having an inflated ego. Trust that your contributions are always valued. When you know how your Ego Centre functions, you will be able to cruise through life with a sense of self-confidence.

DEFINED

A defined Ego Centre gives you a constant stream of motivation and you can control your energy resources with your consistent willpower. When you commit to a project or person, you will always have enough energy to see it through. You keep your promises and if there is something you want, you will have it. You have a strong work ethic and manage your own resources brilliantly, but do not place too many expectations on colleagues who might not share your conviction or power. Be aware when you are pushing others too hard or slip into an inflated sense of your own importance.

Being competitive is not a negative quality, neither is being labelled 'too much'. You have the energy to inspire a stadium full of people, although there might be a few who are intimidated by you. Do not be afraid to hold yourself to high expectations. Sometimes you feel like you are the only person who can do a job and that everyone is relying on you, however, do not push yourself too hard or force an opportunity. You bring so much power to every situation, so acknowledge the true value of your contributions.

UNDEFINED

While your undefined Ego Centre means you are naturally more inconsistent with your willpower and motivation, when you are in alignment you still know that you can complete a task and honour your time and energy. You do this without pushing yourself – or others – and appreciate that you do not need to know what you want all the time. In contrast, when you are out of alignment you might constantly feel you have something to prove or underestimate your own value. You might feel a pressure to earn your place, which could force you into comparisons with other people or an urge to prove yourself that might end in burnout. Trust that you have your own unique energy, and that you are worthy and valuable just as you are.

Sometimes you may struggle with low self-esteem. Remember, this is not who you are, it is a feeling that has stirred up simply because you lack definition on one area of your Body Graph. If you follow your Strategy and Authority, you can still realize all your dreams. The universe wants you to experience abundance, love and support, so believe that you deserve the best.

AFFIRMATIONS: I am worthy and have nothing to prove.

SPLENIC

Splenic is the most ancient energy Centre and connects us to a primitive level of existence, but it can warn you of dangers in today's world, too. It is responsible for how you work out what is safe (or not), fear, intuition, health, bodily awareness and spontaneity. Physically, it is associated with your immune system, lymph and spleen. Your Splenic Centre is the source of much wisdom. It is also one of the most subtle energies. If you have Splenic Authority, you will have read that it whispers, not shouts – it gives intuitive guidance.

DEFINED

Your constant access to the spleen's intelligence and intuition gives you a reliable direct line to its quiet messages. When you are living in alignment with a defined Splenic Centre, you will trust your body's intuition and can make instant judgements about what – or who – is safe. You live in the present with a secure sense of belonging and are not afraid to take risks. Your biggest challenge is strengthening your communication with your spleen and listening, as it does not often repeat its messages. When you are out of alignment, you will find you ignore your intuition or miss those quiet notifications. You may find fear holds you back from trusting your own judgement. Most people with a defined Splenic Centre are blessed with strong immune systems but do not forget to attend regular medicals.

UNDEFINED

The lack of a constant link to your safety instincts can lead you to become afraid in many areas of your life. You might feel unsafe alone or have worries about losing people you love to illness or accident. Insecurity might mean you cling onto things, places or people that no longer serve you and you may hold back from living your truth, from fear of negative consequences, judgement from others and unknown outcomes.

If you have an undefined Splenic Centre, you also magnify the fears of others. However, if you can confront your worries head on, you will find a release. You feel the pain of the world intensely and can become dependent on people with defined spleens, although these people sometimes push you to make decisions. Instead look to your Strategy and Authority to guide you. When you are in alignment, you will be able to trust your intuition and release any worries about facing your critics or taking on responsibility. You *can* do it.

AFFIRMATION: I release fear and trust myself to know what is best for me.

SOLAR PLEXUS

This motor energy Centre is physically linked to the nervous system, lungs, pancreas, prostate and kidneys. Your solar plexus guides the way you process emotions and awareness, plus the drive to feel and connect. It is how you experience all life's highs and lows. Consider that half the world's population are emotionally defined, so are living on a random wave of highs and lows. The other half, meanwhile, are undefined, which means they live out the feelings anyway! Emotions are running particularly high as we head into the Age of Aquarius (see page 5) and people rise up against continued war, inequality, inequity and injustice. Whether it is something you are experiencing or amplifying, sitting with your feelings will help you learn from them, rather than running away from them or being ruled by them. Work towards cultivating emotional maturity and you will find a stronger connection to your inner spirit, consciousness, passion and desire through your Solar Plexus Centre.

DEFINED

As you live out your own emotional wave, remember to make decisions from an emotionally neutral position and try to remove any labels from how you are feeling. Your mood is not 'good' or 'bad', it just is. Your unbounded creativity means you can see situations from many perspectives and you are able to confront hard truths. When you are living in alignment with a defined Solar Plexus Centre, you can cultivate deep emotional intelligence, developing maturity and resilience through accepting and embracing the highs and lows of your waves. You will be able to find clarity through your intensity and your passion makes you incredibly seductive, not just romantically. If you are out of alignment, you may be unaware of your feelings or find external means to justify impulsive and emotionally charged decisions.

UNDEFINED

As you are susceptible to experiencing amplified versions of all the emotions from people around you, remain aware of your own feelings, as well as what you are simply sampling from nearby. Being around particularly emotional people could leave you feeling like *you* are emotional too, so practise shifting out of those feelings and into a neutral place of observation. However someone else is feeling, it is not your responsibility. When you are unaligned, you can start to identify with those emotions that are not your own. You can be held back by fear of rejection and disappointment, and so you avoid confrontation. You would rather say nothing than cause upset. Instead, practise reflecting those emotions back on the other person with a compassionate reminder that you can sense they are feeling angry, frustrated or sad. You have a wonderful gift of being able to support others' emotions through empathy and the ability to discern the difference between your emotions and theirs. When you tune into being led by your Strategy and Authority, you will be able to put your needs and desires to the fore and release any worries of confrontation to move on with your life.

AFFIRMATION: I observe the emotions around me, but I do not let them define me.

SACRAL

How you use the motor energy that generates life-force, sexuality and fertility comes from your Sacral Centre. It will guide you through life, based on instant responses that allow you to work, move, create, have children and take on long-term projects, such as house renovations. Physically linked to the sexual organs, 70 per cent of humans have defined a Sacral Centre.

DEFINED

If you are Generator or Manifesting Generator (MG) with a defined Sacral Centre, you might be described as a Sacral Being. You are powered by a consistent motor that only knows 'yes' and 'no', or 'on' and 'off'. It does not recognize grey areas or 'maybe'. If your Sacral Centre has the energy to engage with a person or project, it will burst into life. You need plenty of outlets where you can use up your excess energy, or you will end up feeling more drained. When you are energized, you light up the room with your firework energy. When you are not, you stagnate a whole space.

You have an internal energy resource that will power you through the day but be careful not to give away energy to things you feel you 'should' do. If you sacrifice yourself for others, in however small a task, you could bring out feelings of your Not-Self Theme. When you are in alignment, your tenacity and positivity will energize everyone around you. Listen to your internal guidance to lead you to projects that you will be passionate about.

UNDEFINED

You need to get your daily fuel from other people. If you have a professional relationship with Generators or MGs who have defined Sacral Centres, it could be a particularly brilliant partnership. Make sure you set boundaries to avoid getting too tired and remember to rest when you have had enough. Living out of alignment with an undefined Sacral Centre will see you working too hard or trying to keep up with others. You may be guilty of always saying 'yes' or pushing yourself too far. You might believe that if you do not do it, it will not get done. You have a real sense of responsibility to other people and things. Tune into your inner guidance and start saying 'no' when you feel pressured. Manifestors, Projectors and Reflectors with undefined Sacral Centres can experience huge energy rushes when around those with defined Sacral Centres. However, remember you are not meant to live with such intense energy all the time. If you need a short boost of productivity, go for it, but always make sure you release yourself from the energetic pressure at the end of the day or it could lead to burnout or overwhelm.

AFFIRMATION: I have healthy boundaries and always rest before I am tired.

ROOT

The pressure Centre and motor energy Centre combine to propel you to take action and move forward. Your Root Centre guides your adaptability and reactions to stress and is physically connected to the adrenal glands. How you pace yourself, as you move through the world, will depend on your Root Centre's energy.

DEFINED

When you find yourself in a stressful situation, others see you as a calm and grounded presence, ready to overcome any challenge. You work well under pressure and your consistency means you get the job done. You work through tasks at your own pace and have a rhythm that sets the pace for your colleagues. A defined Root Centre gives you an internal momentum that continually moves you forward, evolving and achieving greatness. You have an intrinsic understanding of how long a task will take, which means you can manage timelines. For you, a defined Root Centre means you take stress as it is – as energy that is neither 'good' nor 'bad', but simply an impetus to get something done.

However, when you are out of alignment, you may find you create your own stress by ignoring your Strategy and Authority and getting bogged down by menial tasks. You might also find resistance if you put pressure on others to meet unrealistic expectations. Try to avoid unimportant tasks and concentrate on projects that instantly spark your energy.

UNDEFINED

Your undefined Root Centre leaves you open to receiving pressure. Sometimes this can act as fuel to get a job done quickly; you often speed through tasks simply to lift the pressure of expectation. However, at other times this external pressure makes you overwhelmed and restless. You can get lost in the feeling that there is always something more to do and start skipping breaks and essential rest. When you trust you can get something done, without forcing yourself, you will always find the best results. Living in alignment will show you that not all pressures are yours – you may be taking in others' stresses – so remember to be discerning.

During quieter times, you may believe that you are lazy or unmotivated. Be aware these also are not your own emotions or feelings. Because you have an inconsistent connection to your Root Centre's energy, you are not designed to do everything (despite feeling you must shoulder all the responsibility, achieve, find your purpose and do more). Overworking yourself leaves you vulnerable to panic attacks, anxiety and depression, so find a stress-release technique that you can rely on. Meditation, exercise or being outside in nature are all excellent options. While you can borrow energy from others to carry you through a high-pressure period, you should always release it at the end of the day by spending time alone. And remember, it is not realistic for you to always have this momentum; it is not a weakness to ask for help and everything will get done when it needs to.

AFFIRMATIONS: I ground myself and release the pressure to do everything.

PROFILES

PROFILES

From schooldays onwards, we come across so many quizzes that reveal your personality type. In Human Design, you do not need to answer any questions. You can find your Profile within your Chart. Each Profile line has a distinct personality of its own and the six Profiles can be arranged in 12 different combinations, depending on the order of the numbers (and whether they relate to how others see you, or what you are on the inside).

Your Human Design Profile is shown as a fraction of two numbers, which represent how you appear to others and how you see yourself. Your Profile is your conscious and unconscious personality type and is calculated from the position of your Personality Sun (on the right of your chart) and your Design Sun (on the left). The numbers after the decimal point make up your unique mix. The number from the right side (the personality side) denotes your conscious traits, the elements you are aware of in your inner self, which come first, followed by the design side (left), which are unconscious traits and how others may see you. Sometimes unconscious traits come as a huge surprise or are hard for you to recognize in yourself, although they might be clear as day to others.

The people around you may interpret your personality in a different way to your own feelings and intentions, yet it makes sense that you would keep your inner self more private, only revealing it to your closest friends and trusted family members. Knowing the difference between your conscious and unconscious Profile lines can give you deeper insight into how best to approach tricky situations and, in turn, can give you learnings on how to show up as your most authentic self throughout your entire life. This knowledge could also help you gain balance in relationships and clarity in your work life. Although you have two sides to your personality, they are not mixed equally inside you; you are designed to have a perfect combination of archetypes for your unique life.

You can also discover your compatibility in love and business relationships through your Profiles. Some people's energies mix together perfectly, while others clash. Likewise, some Profiles are better placed to coexist in harmony. Although there are many other elements that influence your entire Human Design, understanding your Profile will help you navigate any sticking points. There are six Profile archetypes.

My Profile is

---

1 THE INVESTIGATOR

You are here to seek out knowledge. You always want to uncover the truth of every situation. You are on a mission to understand everything, including what makes other people tick. You have a steely inner strength. You always make sure you are fully prepared (and have all the information) before you head into any new situation. You want and need to do all your research before making a decision. You are curious and creative, helping people around you by providing a solid base of knowledge for others to learn from.

2 THE HERMIT

You have so many gifts and skills that come naturally to you, *so* naturally you do not even know you have them! You love to spend time alone and need space around you to deep dive into your talents and hone your skillset. Because your talents are so normal for you, often you need others to remind you just how rare and magical your gifts are. These people will bring you out of your shell, but you already have a magnetic energy that attracts people to you. You excel when you can teach what you already know.

3 THE MARTYR

Your inclination is to explore everything yourself, make discoveries and come to your own conclusions, regardless of others' advice. You always want to experiment with life and see that making mistakes is actually a great way to learn, even though you might sometimes be on the receiving end of blame. You always share your wisdom and learnings from these experiments along the way. You may go through many jobs, relationships or locations before you realize they are not right for you and you move on. The third line shows inbuilt resilience, which allows you to evolve.

4 THE OPPORTUNIST

You make wonderful connections throughout life and instinctively know who is right or wrong for your circle. Your life is all about relationships and connecting people, but you have more discernment simply becoming an unconditional friend to all. You understand that the best opportunities come through your network and have built a strong community. It may be large or small, either way, you always value quality over quantity. You place more faith in recommendations, rather than in an online search. Sometimes you give out more than you receive, so remember to cultivate your boundaries. You are a deep and authentic communicator and love stable, intimate environments.

5 THE HERETIC

You are the person people turn to problem solve and come up with practical solutions that result in a happy ending for all. Sometimes you feel people do not get the real you and often project their own thoughts onto you as your energy contains a projection field. Others may make assumptions about your motives, which do not chime with your beliefs or intentions. Sometimes others expect you to save the day, when it is something you cannot save. Granted, the fifth line is imbued with a saviour essence and you want everyone to feel free, but only get involved if it is an issue aligned with your Strategy and Authority. You are also seen as a liberator, but you cannot always fix everyone's problems, so stay away if it does not feel right.

6 THE ROLE MODEL

Up until age 30, you live life through experimentation and are defined as a third line – the Martyr – because you are busy trying everything out. From ages 30 to 50, you settle into your sixth line and analyze all your experiences. All the while, others are watching how you do this. Then, from around age 50, you move into true role-model mode. You know exactly what your experiences are and can share wisdom about them to the world. Your insights will guide and inspire all those around you as you show, guide and give others something to aspire to. The sixth line can absolutely be successful before you hit 50, but after this point you will ease into greater confidence and awareness, and really shine. Some may describe you as an old soul.

These six archetypes, or starting points, combine in a number of ways, depending on whether they are part of your personality line (your conscious traits) or your design line (your unconscious traits). Each of the 12 possible combinations are explored below.

1/3 THE INVESTIGATOR/THE MARTYR

Have you ever succumbed to imposter syndrome? Banish those feelings. You know exactly what you are talking about because you have experienced life firsthand. You understand there is always more to learn – you are a lifelong student – but this means you are also brilliantly placed to become a mentor because you are always learning new things, absorbing knowledge from others and testing your findings.

You could be described as an expert in your field, although you will likely never believe you are enough. (You *are*.) You love discovering things for yourself, but you need to balance your opposing Profile sides, which represent wanting to learn cautiously through thorough, considered investigation and a need to experience the newness *right now*. These discoveries could come through your job, watching documentaries or travelling and experiencing different cultures and customs.

In work, you are great at your role, but sometimes your third line means you make mistakes due to experimentation. You are not the Type to go along with the status quo just *because.* You might find yourself starting a role or project before you have thought it through, then when you realize it is not for you, you are gone. Remember, your actions can have a huge impact on other people, so be aware not to leave others hanging. Teaching and sharing your knowledge and skills will excite you.

With other people, you have an excellent radar for feeling when something is not right and have huge empathy. You can spot when someone is lying or being fake. You will often be the person ready to chat to everyone at a party (due to your first line), but as soon as you are done, you are out the door. Likewise, because you are a direct communicator, you will share your thoughts and then... Thank you. Next!

In love you are open and always investigate before you make a commitment to a relationship, although you might have had many relationships due to your restless nature. You have a niggling worry at the back of your mind that you could end up alone, which may make you unconsciously non-committal, even though you dream of a secure relationship (despite a conflicting fear of being restricted). One day you will realize that you are repeating the same patterns in love and find someone who you want to be with forever, will *never* be bored with and reach utter fulfilment at last.

1/4 THE INVESTIGATOR/THE OPPORTUNIST

Making introductions, sharing tips and recommendations and dissecting the news with your closest confidantes all ignite your unique personality Profile. Staying up all night reading, watching documentaries or googling a subject you are obsessed with are all classic 1/4 traits.

Throughout life, you want to investigate whatever intrigues you and then share your findings with your inner circle. You are curious about human behaviour and want to understand what makes someone tick. Friends describe you as warm and welcoming. You build a circle of beautiful connections: you make everyone open up and they feel comfortable in your presence. When you speak, it is from the heart. However, if someone hurts you, you will shut down completely.

In work, you are a strong, powerful authority. People love learning from you, however, you must listen to your Strategy for the right time to share your knowledge. You do not need to have lived through a situation to give your thoughts, but the more you share, the more successful you become – and fast. Surround yourself with other leaders who can mentor you and then become a mentor yourself. When working on something you are passionate about, you are focused and take risks. You are an innovative team-player with entrepreneurial flair who loves being recognized for your unique skills. You have more recognition and admirers than you will ever realize, so your best opportunities will come from your connections.

You need plenty of time alone to be creative and find the balance between your outgoing-yet-discerning first line and your gregarious-but-wary fourth line. That means you are ready to engage with life once you feel secure and understand the whole truth in a situation. You crave control, due to the insecurities in your first line, yet you fear rejection, characterized in your fourth line. Be aware that if you start to spiral into internal thoughts, you risk ignoring the friends around you and retreating into solitude, which can trigger your Not-Self Theme.

Always wondering who the most authentic souls are in a space, if you are pushed to give more than you receive you could burn out. Prioritize relationships where there is a healthy balance and you are supported to be your most authentic self.

2/4 THE HERMIT/THE OPPORTUNIST

There are two contrasting sides to your personality, but that does not mean you have to choose – you can be both, depending on your energy and the situation. Sometimes you want to hole up at home alone, while at other times you are happy to chat all night, although you will always prefer small gatherings over big occasions. Rather than initiating conversations, you will be found waiting for people to come to you... and people will *always* come to you. You have an air of mystery that draws others in. Although some perceive you as shy, this is just a filter to ensure you share yourself only with people worthy of your unique energy.

You are an introverted extrovert and susceptible to tiredness. When it is time to cheerlead your friends and family or share your mission, you need your precious energy. You find it difficult to see your own gifts – and faults – so listen to feedback that may reveal clarity. Others see you more clearly than you see yourself, so having a close circle of friends around you will support you, give you strength and help you define your purpose. Your friends would say you are easy-going and brilliant at holding space for those who need it.

In work you could become a wise leader and instructor. You have an intuitive understanding of other people's needs, although sometimes you can get *too* close to others. Be aware that you have the potential to be overly submissive, become unduly influenced, and take your identity from those you are around, and are even susceptible to imitating others. The positive side of these traits is that you listen intently in conversation and are able to gain insights into your own self through others' knowledge. If you are interrupted when involved in an engaging task, you can become furious. If you are provoked, you have a mean streak.

Throughout your journey, you have a driving force deep within you, which will help you bring your purpose in life to reality. Highly creative, 2/4 Profiles border on genius.

You have so much love to give, although this is balanced by an unconscious fear of rejection and conscious worries that you are giving too much. Being authentic is the way you will shine in life and remember to always trust yourself and your inner guidance.

2/5 THE HERMIT/THE HERETIC

You have so many gifts, but you do not see them, despite others being magnetized to you and fascinated by your talents. You are more than happy to stay curled up at home, due to your second line (nothing makes you happier than plans being cancelled), but you equally love to help others, which means showing up in the outside world. Use your Strategy and Authority to work out when your unique problem-solving skills are required and when you should steer clear of tricky situations.

You do not feel like a born leader, yet you have buckets of charisma, which means others may put you on a pedestal. You deserve to be there. The gifts you have been nurturing need a moment in the spotlight and you have a wonderful opportunity to use your influence to improve the world. Just be aware that you do not allow a moment of glory to feed your ego or, conversely, slip you into imposter syndrome. You may be led by a need for status, although you worry that you are only appreciated for outside appearances and not your authentic self. As long as you stay true to yourself and do not try to shape others' opinions of you, you will find harmony.

You are dedicated to your job, despite moving between many roles. You are full of brilliant ideas and will receive praise during your career. You are a creative soul. You have no idea how valued you are in the workplace and often end up in a crisis management role, both in your work and in your friendships. When you can, you love learning and practising new skills.

Sometimes you worry that you will never meet someone who will be your perfect match; it is likely you will have only a couple of truly meaningful relationships in your lifetime. You are fussy – and rightly so – but believe that you will find someone who can honour your needs. Do not be afraid to outline exactly what you want in a partner. It is what you deserve.

You are braver than you will ever realize. Although you are deeply drawn to philanthropy, you also need your own space. Move on from craving approval from others and get ready for a wonderful future, if you can believe it for yourself.

3/5 THE MARTYR/THE HERETIC

You have experienced hardship, but you treat every 'mistake', misfortune, heartbreak or frustration as an opportunity for further learnings (and excellent anecdotes). Life for a 3/5 Profile is a wonderful experiment and you cannot wait to share all your experiences. People describe you as loveable, witty and relatable – they are fascinated to hear your take on how to live – and you have an aura of lightness and joy.

If there is a chance to go skydiving, bungee jumping or swimming with sharks, you will take it. You want to do everything just to see how it feels. The more positive you are in your day to day, the more wonderful opportunities will flow to you. However, be aware that the more you hold onto low moments, the more they will show up in your life. Your third line represents gathering wisdom while your fifth line is how you impart it to others. You have true knowledge, from living those experiences, and need to share it with many types of people.

You are busy in life and in work. You may build a business, or businesses, as an entrepreneur. You love trying new things and are a natural mentor. You may write a book or autobiography, or find other creative ways to make money. Keep a journal to remind you of your accomplishments and the compliments you receive (there will be many). You are the first to call out injustices and are always ready to challenge authority. You want to make the world a better place for everyone.

Routine is a drag. You are excellent at drawing people to you, but you may have trouble committing as you need freedom. You need a partner who will understand (or share) your yearning to travel and will always cheerlead you. If someone needs help, your sensitivity will alert you. You are the person to take charge in a crisis. You do not hold grudges but when *you* need support, you never let on. At some point, living at break-neck speed will be too much. You will start to crave a quiet life, even if you find it hard to truly settle. Do not worry, your future will *still* be fascinating. For you, a life well-lived is always about the journey.

3/6 THE MARTYR/THE ROLE MODEL

If the first 30 years of your life felt like riding a rollercoaster, you are living a classic 3/6 Profile, although you are actually experiencing life as a 3/3 Profile (read that section too for more insight). Later in life, you will segue into a position of authority and as a role model; you may find yourself placed on a pedestal, with everyone hanging off your every word. You fascinate people and command attention, however you will be typically humble (although you know that you have earned this position). Born with inner wisdom, as you go through life, your experiences will educate you even more. You will understand that you have an innate responsibility to those around you but wear it with a relaxed air – that is the way you balance your two personality lines.

Until you are 30, you will thirst to try so many things. Clarity over those elements will not come until later in life, when you will bring order to the chaos you have experienced. Those learnings will give authenticity to your knowledge as people will trust you more, knowing that you have lived. Be aware that some situations require you to just observe, rather than do. Remember making 'mistakes' is natural, although you still do not like them. Avoid the trap of perfection and practise acceptance. You will explore many ways to make money through sharing your knowledge, entrepreneurship or moving from 'doing' jobs to directing roles. Travel excites you, as does meeting new people and experimenting with new hobbies.

Your life is one of contrasts. As you get older you will crave peace and quiet, but there will still be opportunities for adventures and excitement. You will build a home you love, yet still yearn to travel. Trust your Strategy and Authority for the awareness of when it is right to indulge in the different parts of yourself and know that you never need to choose only one path. You can alternate depending on how you feel.

In love, you might think you do not need a relationship. You are tough! Your third line is naturally non-committal, but deep down you crave the safety of someone who wants to look after you and will honour your need for space. Your sixth line will balance your ever-present restlessness and know that your unconscious self has endless insight that your conscious mind will not see. If you ever feel trapped, it is likely that you are not engaging your energy in an aligned way, in love or in life.

Whether you are experiencing a moment of calm or travelling at lightning speed, your experiments and learnings will make you a trusted authority on life.

4/1 THE OPPORTUNIST/THE INVESTIGATOR

You have a very particular and precise way of living. Your heart's desire is set to guide you towards your destiny. This is because, out of all the Profiles, yours is rare and is the only one that is fixed. In Human Design, someone's fate is set by the 64 gates on their Body Graph, but yours is set by just one of these. This means your course in life is predetermined. You are the only Profile with a Juxtaposition Incarnation Cross (which is discussed in Chapter 9). Life will propel you towards your destiny. In anything you do, your sense of purpose is deeply engrained; if you live out of accordance with this, you will suffer deeply (for example, if you have to relocate for a job or change relationships). You may find life is doubly tough because of this, but throughout all these challenges, your true nature remains happy and light.

Your mission may make you inflexible and you are ready to live life alone but know that the right people *will* come into your life. Never feel that you need to change to fit someone else's idea of a relationship. Your Authority will guide you to people who are worthy of your engagement (clue: those who respect you and appreciate your individualism). Conditioning may make you feel heavy, particularly when you see others leading flexible lives, but continue to hold your head and standards high.

Work – which can be different to your purpose – may see you involved in teaching or mentoring. You love to study all there is to know about human nature. You give 100 per cent in whatever you do. When you find a subject that inspires you, you can border on obsession and are prone to mental exhaustion. Your mind has a unique way of organizing knowledge, which means you can see the world in black and white. Remember not everyone thinks like you. Be ready to filter out opinions to show you the truth in situations.

Make sure you always have plenty of time alone to reflect and process: this is how you grow. Sometimes you may undergo huge change, and while living a life that serves your destiny can feel hard, being in alignment can help you find elements of genius in your fate.

4/6 THE OPPORTUNIST/THE ROLE MODEL

You are the social secretary in your friendship group. Parties and events revolve around your presence. Your aura is charming and you radiate joy. You are a natural entertainer and will have the room hooked on your anecdotes and stories. Everyone looks up to you. You are an early adopter. You are the first to try out or even initiate trends. You act as a guide in groups and gatherings, whether IRL or online, providing genuine concern and support.

Friends would say you are warm and wise with a huge heart, although you can shy away from sharing too much for fear of making yourself vulnerable (even though you will be loved even more for your authenticity). At times, you may push people away before they get the chance to leave you, but they never will. Feelings of rejection or failure can make you retreat into solitary protection mode. You *want* to be accepted and can try too hard to be liked, but you do not have to! Your circle is huge and if you can move away from doing everything yourself (you can be a bit of a control freak), you will see you have so many supporters, ready and willing to help. You can be prone to anxious moments, which may lead to burnout, so build time for meditation and self-care (or book a holiday). Remember, mistakes are how you grow (even though you are capable of perfection) and so it is time to stop being so hard on yourself.

At work, you have a drive that cheerleads for *everyone* to succeed. While you love being part of a team, you gravitate to roles where you can oversee a project as a consultant or mentor rather than a 'doer'. You see everything and can offer a wise perspective, and although you are uncannily right about most things, you will benefit from guidance from your Strategy and Authority. Growth and opportunities come to you through your circle of connections.

In your younger years, you may experience many ups and downs, likely due to romance, but keep your heart open and optimistic. After your Saturn returns (once you reach your thirties), you will find a way to settle. You do not need to do anything for the universe to pour abundance on you and your sixth line gives you the opportunity to make your dreams reality.

5/1 THE HERETIC/THE INVESTIGATOR

People flock to you for your unique problem-solving skills. You have a solution to every issue, although sometimes you feel pressured to fix everything. You hate to let others down. Remember, if they depend on you, that is their issue. Your worth should not be based on others' expectations and you need to be appreciated for all the other talents you have (there are many) particularly in romantic relationships, where you can take on a rescuing role.

You are destined to take on leadership positions and have sense of responsibility attached to your Profile. But be wary as this can have two sides. Too much responsibility can tire you out, yet too little leaves you feeling inefficient. When you use your energy on dull projects, you will run out of steam for the things that *will* ignite you. To help you find alignment, only get involved with things that truly inspire you.

Your role and title at work defines you; you need a job that serves your interests. You may be drawn to volunteer work. Ignore any nagging thoughts that you are not strong enough, your skills are always trustworthy, although be aware that trying to fulfil others' misaligned expectations can tarnish your reputation. Listen to your Strategy and Authority to know when to speak your truth.

You always need challenges that energize you and 5/1 Profiles have a lifelong love of learning. Never dumb down to get others to like you and own your skills. One of your unique gifts is understanding other people's processes and you are meticulous in your research. Your referees would describe you as thorough and dependable. However, while you can take on the world, you struggle with defining your own self. Behind the strong image you project, who is the real you? You like to impress people with your sharp wit and you love intellectual discussions (the more controversial the better). You are excellent at rescuing people, but who is there to rescue you?

Schedule plenty of time alone for self-reflection, to learn and to strengthen your natural air of mystery. When you disappear, you will always be missed, along with your precious ability to guide the world to a better future.

5/2 THE HERETIC/THE HERMIT

It's always been in your nature to help anyone struggling. You want to fix the faults of the world, (and you're often the best person to solve a problem) but sometimes you need to step back. It might not be right for you to get involved and you also need plenty of time alone to protect your own energies. Despite your saviour status you are also prone to overthinking (you can spiral into questioning your own genius and abilities) which may leave you feeling overwhelmed and disheartened. To counter this, you need to rest and recharge. At the end of the day you often want to retreat into your home. Spending time alone, cancelling plans in favour of relaxation or having deep one-on-one conversations are your idea of a good time.

You'll always strive to do things on your own terms and other people are intrigued by your methods and approach. You may have an urge to use your unique gifts, fearing you'll lose them otherwise, but remember to honour your Strategy and only get involved when you're truly motivated or triggered by your authority. If you feel pressured by others, ask if you're putting extra pressure on yourself, too. You have so much potential for greatness (you'll have plenty of opportunities to fulfil this) and sticking to your own ideals and highest values will help you achieve your best purpose.

If you spend time worrying about fitting in at social events, or about how you appear to others, release those thoughts. You'll always be able to slot naturally into any situation. Those around you will be captivated by your presence. Don't be mean to yourself if you make a perceived mistake, just keep studying the projects that inspire you, reading and expressing yourself creatively.

In relationships you can feel frustrated by the seemingly slow pace of others. You'll benefit from your partner's feedback, but need to allow yourself to be truly vulnerable to receive it. When you are able acknowledge your own brilliance, others will hold your talents in high esteem too. Don't wait for recognition, get your skills known and out into the world.

6/2 THE ROLE MODEL/THE HERMIT

Even as a child, people probably noticed you were wise beyond your years and had so much clarity on how things could be made better. And as an adult? You have likely grown up into exactly who you wished you would become. Now you have the chance to action your childhood plans. You have huge goals (which *can* be achieved) and consistently high standards (which *will* be met). You have sparkling opportunities for greatness. Direct your energy towards becoming as extraordinary as you can; you have superior gifts compared to society's regular benchmarks.

At work, you sometimes feel frustrated that your colleagues are not as accomplished or as fast as you. Instead of wondering why you bother when no one else does, remember you do everything to your best ability for yourself, not others. Your perfectionist qualities exist because you have the potential to be exceptional, and although you are truly amazing, remember to stay humble. Sometimes you are prone to micromanaging your colleagues, so delegate tasks only to those you trust. While you are supportive and a kind mentor, you are not here to hold anyone's hand. You can take charge of any situation, but too much responsibility can feel like a chore. If you *have* taken on too much, do not blame anyone else for your choices.

As a sixth line Profile, until you reach 30, you may feel like you are living in a pinball machine. It can be a wild ride. Remember each test will give you wisdom *and* a little push to keep getting better. Everyone is waiting to hear your wisdom, yet you always crave more knowledge. Remain optimistic and rise above petty drama. Your second line means you sometimes want to step back from a situation, in which case check in with yourself. Is it just because you cannot be bothered to get involved? Unless you put yourself out there, you may miss some of life's most amazing opportunities.

In romance, do not make assumptions about your partner or nitpick their perceived faults. You tend to want to 'improve' people but trying to control someone will not end well. Even when you are with someone, you need privacy and space to recharge alone, especially as the wider world is always watching you. After you turn 30, you will also need more time alone. Consider ways that you can share your life on your own terms. You have incredible talents and can guide the world to a better place as long as you – and all your gifts – are visible.

6/3 THE ROLE MODEL/THE MARTYR

Nothing about your life will be mundane and you thrive through extreme experiences or risk-taking. Your unique Human Design means you *can* have it all, although remember that even the most exciting lives involve some dull moments – we all have to do laundry! Just do not let these mundane moments get your down. Keep your sense of wonder throughout every task. You have an inbuilt ability to make your own fun; this is how you can help others *and* make your whole life wonderful.

Throughout life, you may find you are constantly receiving messages from the universe, which guide you to keep searching. You are meant to experience the world in all its technicolour glory. These messages are reminders of all that is out there ready for you to relish. For you, experiences *are* enjoyment. If you are drawn to something, you do not need to justify that attraction with a reason, just believe that it will reap rewards at some point in your life or it may help define your purpose.

In work, you thrive when you are handed responsibility and have a hunger to climb the career ladder. Your goals might include starting your own business, making a difference or taking a seat in the boardroom. Making money is a driver for you. The way you learn is through trial and error, although you hate making 'mistakes', particularly if you make them before you turn 30. You may struggle in the earlier years because you believe perfection is the only option. As you get older, you will view your 'mistakes' as learnings that have given you knowledge and a chance to experiment. In turn, this gives you relatability and depth in all your interactions.

In love, you need a partner who is equally adventurous as you and who you can completely trust. You have likely worried that you will never find someone who lives up to your wishlist, but you will reach turning points at 18, 30 and 50 years old. You are always looking for people who you classify as being as vibrant as you and who challenge your thinking and share intellectual ideas. You have so much wisdom yourself, so do not forget to share your own thoughts and recommendations within your circle.

You are fun yet wise. Continue to search for inner enjoyment, while on the outside it appears that you have your life totally together! If you are a 6/3 Profile, remember that you can – and will – experience it all.

NEXT-LEVEL LEARNING

NEXT-LEVEL LEARNING

While you can reach a deep level of understanding of your own Human Design through exploring your Type, Strategy, Authority, Centres and Profile, the next level of learning runs deeper. So far, we have covered the elements of Human Design that will make the biggest difference in your day-to-day life. However, there are not enough pages in this book to reveal everything about Human Design; it is up to you to move into the next level of learning, depending on what you feel you need to know.

Ra Uru Hu received (and transmitted) the system, teaching Human Design to practitioners across the world, but he also advised that we each must experiment with our Design. In other words, you have to put in the work.

While the Human Design system includes some elements consistent with scientific structure, there can be no fully definitive framework as we are still all individuals. While Types, Authorities and Profiles are classified, you may recognize elements of yourself in some classifications, but not necessarily identify with everything listed under that title. However, if any particular sections have intrigued or resonated with you so far, you might want to deep dive into the meaning of other parts of Human Design, which can reveal even more specific traits.

You may yearn to know your purpose (if so, start with your Incarnation Cross) or discover your unique gifts (they are found in your Gates and Channels). Perhaps you need to understand more about how your mind is aligned with your energies and where you should live or how you should eat for optimum health? You will decode that information from your Variables (see page 201). If you need further guidance around the different energies discussed in Chapter 7, your Definition will reveal how your Centres are combined.

INCARNATION CROSS

Your Incarnation Cross is deciphered from the positions of your Sun and Earth, combined with your Profile, and reveals themes and learnings that you may experience during your life. On a practical level, you will find the numbers that denote your Incarnation Cross on the Sun and Earth lines of the Personality and Design columns of your Body Graph.

Human Design offers 192 basic Incarnation Crosses, as well as 768 specific Incarnation Crosses. Each Cross contributes 70 per cent of the consistent energy – and therefore influence – to both yourself and your journey. It is a big deciding factor on how your Human Design plays out, because your Sun and Earth play such a significant role for each of us. Revealing your true Incarnation Cross, and therefore your life's purpose, tends to emerge once you have built a strong foundation and found your passions and direction, which usually occurs between the ages of 38 and 42. Combined with living your Human Design, this knowledge will allow you to leave a legacy, which you will find through your true purpose, but it is important to know that your Incarnation Cross does not correspond with something as simple as revealing your destiny.

A reminder: your purpose is not your job, it is how you apply your unique energy to every situation in your life. When you live your Human Design through your Authority and Strategy, you will start to attract opportunities that let you live in the right energy, and you will likewise bring that energy to all your interactions and therefore define your purpose.

As there are so many Incarnation Crosses, we cannot go through each of them individually. However, these Crosses are divided into three types and some – although not all – have four versions which represent the Quarter of Life Themes. After the phrase that describes your Incarnation Cross (for example, 'Right Angle Cross of Rulership'), there are numbers which correspond with the Gates on your Body Graph. Each type of Cross has a specific energy and direction that will, of course, represent you when combined with the rest of your Design.

My Incarnation Cross is

_____

RIGHT ANGLE CROSS = PERSONAL

Throughout life, you are on a personal journey that sees you continually learning about yourself. That does not mean you are following a selfish path, rather living a journey that allows you to become truly enlightened about your own individuality. In turn, your own path can deeply influence others. You may become a guide or be held up as an example for others. When you are living authentically and aligned to your own Design, it will vastly improve the lives of others. People are drawn to you when you are living in harmony, but you will slip out of alignment when you are expected to conform or are pressured to live up to other people's – or society's – expectations.

LEFT ANGLE CROSS = INTERPERSONAL

Your life lessons come to light through relationships. You find the most opportunities for growth through interacting with others and you find your role defined by guiding people or being guided yourself. Your purpose may be combined with another's. Be aware that if you feel you are in a relationship where you are giving more than you are given, or the other way round, switch things up to find balance. The best shared journeys provide you with profound growth and deeper opportunities to gain wisdom, which will be amplified through your partner's accompaniment. Your life will prove that while we are all individuals, together we are stronger.

JUXTAPOSITION CROSS = FIXED

You differ from other Crosses as your path takes a straight line towards a goal that was set before your birth. Juxtaposition Crosses are rare, and while you might struggle with the fixed themes in your life, your destination could impart a huge influence on others. You thrive through routine and have a methodical approach when challenges come your way, although be aware that too much rigidity is not healthy for you. Finding balance between flexibility and your fixed purpose is essential to help you live your best life. Stay steady and your life could have more impact on the wider world than you could ever imagine.

GATES AND CHANNELS

A deep dive into your Gates and Channels will reveal so much about the way you deal with life, express your emotions and uncover your unique gifts. You have your specific Type and defined Centres because of your defined Gates, which will all have been activated by the planetary placements before and at the time of your birth.

On your Body Graph, defined Gates are the numbers dotted around the triangular, square or diamond-shaped energy Centres, which are coloured in. Each Gate corresponds to the 64 hexagrams of the I Ching *and* the 64 codons found in human DNA. Human Design believes this is more than just mere coincidence and that the 64 Gates can provide a direct map of our genetic codes. Between those numbers, there are 36 Channels, or lines.

Leading from the defined Gates (the coloured-in numbers), the Channels will either be completely coloured in with one of two shades, half coloured, striped or colourless. If completely coloured in, that is because the Gate is activated in both adjoining energy Centres, meaning it is a defined Channel. The energy of each Gate combines to form an array of sparkling qualities and gifts.

The colours correspond with either shade from the Charts on the sides of your Body Graph, which represent your Personality (conscious experiences) or Design (unconscious traits). Where your Chart is generated from will change the colours, but Personality Channels show conscious traits that you will easily recognize, while Design Channels equate to what you experience unconsciously. Striped Channels mean your Gates are activated on the Personality *and* Design sides (they can be full lines or half lines) and you will find these hold a more prominent position in your Chart and therefore life at large. If you have half lines coloured in, these are Gates and colourless Channels are undefined.

Gates are where we take in (and exert) energy from our Centres. The energy that travels through each Channel is different in turn. Your defined Gates and Channels will combine to characterize your aura and are a consistent energy source. In contrast, your undefined Gates are dormant. They will only switch on their energy when you interact with someone who has the corresponding Centre defined or the planets transit to a position that activates your Gates and Channels.

My Defined Gate is

_____

My Defined Channel is

_____

HOW TO USE YOUR GATES

In life, we are so often advised to strive for what we want, however Human Design encourages you simply to just *be*. You do not need to work on changing your Gates and Channels, they exist perfectly. While you might instantly recognize some of the themes they present, others may not surface until later in your life. Nonetheless, learning about your Gates will you help you gain greater understanding and acceptance about how you operate, how you react, what triggers you and what your skills are. In turn, this will allow you to hold space for those elements in your life. Your defined Gates can be compared to gifts or perhaps a personal toolkit of skills, which show you how you can apply yourself and fulfil your dreams. They are often descriptive and are aligned to an array of areas including intuition, provocation, intimacy or nurture.

You will find maximum fulfilment when you fully utilize those gifts, and not just through work. People who sparkle in life are likely to be using all their defined Gates, and therefore all the gifts they have been given. If you are not 'good' at something, do not strive to become 'better' when it is not something that interests you. Instead, concentrate on the gifts and skills that are already within you. Your Gates show you the talents that you have (which you likely do not even recognize, as they are second nature). Once you allow those qualities into your days, you will attract so much more abundance into your life, as well as into the lives of others. There is a sliding scale for each gift. So, if you have a defined Gate that shows leadership, you could go from leader of a village youth group to amplifying that gift into a role in government or heading up a global business. However, you flex your gifts is up to you, but tapping into them, using them and making them work for you will give you the most satisfaction. You will never need to push for success when you live in alignment with the gifts your Gates have already blessed you with.

The flip side of living in alignment with your Gates is when you feel off, frustrated or are noticing your Not-Self Themes. Returning to the knowledge of your Strategy and Authority can help strengthen your integral characteristics and bring you back into a zone where more opportunities and abundance will flow into your life.

Remember, you do not need to know (or understand) every part of your Chart right away. If you are living in accordance with your Strategy and Authority, when situations occur, you can come back into your learnings to unveil why something might be happening, and how best to navigate your way through it. You will certainly find clues and directions within your Gates and Channels.

DEFINITION

After learning the ways that your energy Centres interact (see Chapter 7), the next level is deciphering how those Centres process energy. This also reveals the ways in which you communicate with others, and yourself. You will have your own unique grouping of energy Centres; this depends on which of your Gates are defined (and which lead to other Centres). You can see which grouping or Definition applies to you on your Body Graph but you will also find your Definition listed on your chart. It will be described as Undefined, Single, Split, Triple Split or Quadruple Split.

As you go through life, your defined Centres will automatically pull you towards those people who also have the same Centres defined. Your aura will search out those who can connect, or bridge, any split areas on your Chart. It is not something you will need to actively do, however, as your energy Centres will navigate you in aligned directions to ensure you find what you may need. While you may be able to learn from interactions with those who bridge your splits, it is important to remember that any potential splits on your Body Graph are there for a greater reason and present new opportunities to gain wisdom or skills. Splits are not intrinsically 'bad' (and definition is not inherently 'good'). They do not necessarily mean you are lacking in any area; you just have a different way of receiving energy.

My Definition is

_____

UNDEFINED

You are a Reflector. As you do not have any defined Centres, you interact with the world in a different energetic manner, which is completely unique to you.

SINGLE

Your defined Centres are connected and create one clear area on your Body Graph. Those with single Definition often find it easy to process information quickly and are quite happy to get on with life themselves. You are often self-sufficient and self-assured. Sometimes you feel that other people are too slow for you, or that you are fine without them. Harnessing the fast flow of your energy comes easily as it moves uninterrupted and is focused on just one section of your Chart.

Aligned – You can go through life feeling confident, independent and more than content to be alone.

Unaligned – Sometimes your single Definition can succumb to conditioning and reveal feelings of isolation and loneliness.

SPLIT

The two groupings of energy Centres within you can sometimes feel like they are both talking at the same time. You may feel that you need to really concentrate or listen more carefully to decipher the messages that your inner voices are sharing. The best way for you to process information is through one-to-one conversations with close confidants. You are drawn to others that have the energy needed to bridge the gap between your two defined areas.

Aligned – You can clearly understand the perspectives of opposing groups and are skilled at encouraging people to co-operate.

Unaligned – Be aware that you do not become over-reliant on another or lose your sense of self when in a relationship.

TRIPLE SPLIT

As you have three clusters of defined Centres, you can take a longer amount of time to deal with all the voices and energy that you are simultaneously facing. There are several splits in your Chart, so you need to spend time around many different people to help bridge them. That means being part of a large team at work, socializing in groups or searching out busy places, such as coffee shops. Bridging those gaps can be a complex process; sometimes you feel your sense of self is lacking as you search for others' energetic input.

Aligned – You thrive in situations where you can problem-solve or incorporate strategic thinking and are open to new ideas.

Unaligned – You may find it hard to make decisions or reach clarity as you feel pulled in many directions from your different Centres.

QUADRUPLE SPLIT

This is a rare Definition. Because you have so many defined Centres, you give out way more energy than you take in. Energetically you are a closed book, but this means you also have a glorious opportunity to impact the world with your unique thinking. You always consider your decisions and often take your time processing your thoughts and feelings, as you have so many factors contributing to them. Quadruple split Definition can sometimes feel like having four different personalities. It can be tricky to allow each area to have its moment, as your energy Centres do not communicate with each other.

Aligned – You can be flexible and adapt well to being with many different groups and types of people.

Unaligned – Sometimes you become dependent on others and may find it hard to set boundaries.

VARIABLES

If you want to know more about how your body processes your food into fuel and how your brain takes in and filters information, this is where you will find the clues. Understanding and acting on your Variables is an advanced level of Human Design. This is the part of your Chart that really needs accuracy regarding your birth time, right down to the exact minute. You can experiment and input different times into your preferred Human Design Chart website or app, but if you do not feel that your Chart resonates with you, not having an accurate birth time might be why.

The depth of what you can learn through investigating your Variables – and how it can benefit your being – is truly epic. Human Design is not something you can master in a weekend (although you can pick up the basic principles, as we have already discovered), but if you want to know more about your unique Human Design and how to improve every aspect of your life, deep dive into your Variables. This small section is just the tip of the iceberg.

We are all individuals. When you know the optimum way for you to thrive, you can concentrate on serving those needs and therefore your aligned Human Design, rather than forcing yourself to do activities or live in a way that grates against your nature. Variables is where you find all the clues to your complete cognitive Human Design, your awareness, and the methods with which you experience all the elements around you.

You will find your Variables at the top of your Chart. They are represented by arrows and are calculated by the positions of your Sun, Earth, and North and South Nodes of the Moon from the exact time of your birth. The arrows on the right of your Chart relate to conscious traits and their placement depends on the Human Design Variables (the arrows on the left), which relate to unconscious elements.

Some Human Design Charts do not list all your Variables, so even if you do not know all of your Variables, you can still live your Human Design successfully and authentically. Personal experimentation and experience – and *always* listening to your Strategy and Authority – will be the simplest way to start living in a more aligned manner.

My Variables are

_____

Digestion

_____

Environment

_____

Perspective

_____

Motivation

_____

DETERMINATION/DIGESTION – TOP LEFT ARROW

This shows the ways in which you should fuel both your body and brain with food and information, depending on which of the six main Determinations you have. From those six main Determinations (Appetite, Taste, Thirst, Touch, Sound and Light) each will have a variation that is Active or Passive, depending on the direction of the arrow in the top left of your Chart.

Appetite – you are designed to take in unprocessed food and follow a simple diet.
Active = Consecutive
Passive = Alternating

Taste – follow your discernment when it comes to choosing the foods, restaurants and brands you are aligned to.
Active = Open
Passive = Closed

Thirst – for your body to process in the right manner, your food and liquid intake needs to be at the correct temperature.
Active = Hot
Passive = Cold

Touch – this relates to where you are eating and how stimulating (or calming) the environment is.
Active = Calm
Passive = Nervous

Sound – noise levels have a huge impact in your processes and can help or hinder your digestion.
Active = High
Passive = Low

Light – the amount of sunlight you are subjected to can affect how you digest your food.
Active = Direct
Passive = Indirect

The above Determinations are all part of the myriad factors that contribute to your unique Human Design. Playing around with what feels good for you is the best way to understand your Variables.

As a general guide, if your arrow for Determination faces left, you will need consistent amounts of food (and a steady stream of snacks). You prefer routine in your mealtimes, so your brain has lots of energy to process situations, and if you miss a meal you will head into hangry mode. You are best placed to eat, and take in information, by focusing on one thing at a time. Structure around your eating habits will see you flourish.

If your arrow for Determination points right, you do not need as much fuel to power through your days. Eating when you are hungry, rather than sticking to set timings works best for you. You can easily switch up mealtimes depending on your commitments. When it comes to information, you take in knowledge without realising it and enjoy mixing up your schedule.

ENVIRONMENT - BOTTOM LEFT ARROW

This suggests the places where your mind and body will thrive. When you are in the right environment, you will have a warm, satisfied feeling that you are *exactly* where you should be. Although you do not need to physically move home to live in your right environment, it is helpful to be able to access that type of environment when it is time to make a big decision or you are going through a challenging period. Sometimes you will need to plan ahead to make sure you are living within or experiencing the specific environment that energizes and uplifts you.

There are six environments: Shores, Valleys, Mountains, Kitchens, Markets and Caves. Understand that they do not correspond to their *exact* dictionary definition and there are many ways you can create that environment, far from the implied location. Each environment has a Variable, which will show whether you are Observed or an Observer and the best way to be in your Environment, depending on your own unique Human Design Chart.

If your arrow points left, you are Observed, which means the correct environment energizes you. When you are in the right space, you cannot help but create, move and do. You enjoy the consistency of routine and being in familiar surroundings is a great comfort for you. It takes a little while for you to settle in a new setting.

If your arrow points right, you are an Observer. Being in your correct environment relaxes you. You will become receptive and open, but you also benefit from spending time in a variety of settings, having a nomadic lifestyle or at least spending plenty of time exploring different countries and cultures. You need to have freedom and plenty of options when it comes to your work location or where you spend your downtime.

Shores – these include beaches and rivers, as well as window seats and other viewpoints looking out over scenery.
Observed = Natural
Observer = Artificial

Valleys – not just physical valleys, these can also be narrow city streets or intimate gatherings.
Observed = Narrow
Observer = Wide

Mountains – as well as geographic hills, this could be a seat on a plane or a flat in a high-rise block.
Observed = Active
Observer = Passive

Kitchens – beyond your actual kitchen, these are also co-working spaces, gyms or urban hubs.
Observed = Wet
Observer = Dry

Markets – any place where there is a multitude of choices, where you can browse the options.
Observed = Internal
Observer = External

Caves - this can be as simple as a restaurant booth or pulling the covers over your head at night in bed.
Observed = Selective
Observer = Blended

PERSPECTIVE – BOTTOM RIGHT ARROW

This Variable shows what you are best to focus on in your life and how you view the world. Consider a time when watching a film with a friend: your individual perceptions could mean it is like you each watched two completely different movies. That is how it is with the Perspective Variable. It is particularly helpful if you can spend time in the right environment, so if you are able to experiment with your location, you will begin to see things in the most helpful way for your Human Design.

There are six views or Perspectives, and six opposite states called Transference. Disruption of your Perspective into Transference is not a negative concept, it will just help you see a situation with balance and remind you to move back into your Signature.

Survival – when you view a situation, you can see exactly what you need to survive in this world.
Transference = Wanting

Possibility – this view means you are always pre-empting what *might* happen in any given situation.
Transference = Probability

Power – you are designed to notice who is successful and which systems and methods work best.
Transference = Personal

Wanting – this means you can identify what your community needs and know how to get it.
Transference = Survival

Probability – you weigh up all the options in a scenario and prepare for the most likely outcome.
Transference = Possibility

Personal – you are focused on experiencing the world through your own reality.
Transference = Power

If you have a left-facing arrow, you like clarity throughout your life. Spending time involved in precise planning and goal setting will help you thrive.

If you have a right-facing arrow, you will fare better by imagining the emotions you feel when you reach your goals. You do not focus on specifics but have a loose idea of what you want from your life ahead.

MOTIVATION – TOP RIGHT ARROW

This is literally what drives you and is concerned with all the inner passions and dreams that inspire you to take action. Your Motivation is a conscious Variable, which means you will notice when you are moving from Motivation into Transference. Note that being in Transference is not a 'bad' thing! As with all of the flip sides in Human Design, such as Not-Self Themes, the state of Transference is simply a helpful nudge to allow you to return to your most aligned life.

Fear – you have a quest to understand everything, to break down its unknown status. When you understand something, it will help you move away from being in a fearful place.
Transference = Need

Hope – this is a Variable that means you will always focus on the positives. You are able to relax and know everything will be okay, without you needing to fix it.
Transference = Guilt

Desire – this is represented by a need to make change and lead your community. You have an inner drive to get involved and make the world a better place for everyone.
Transference = Innocence

Need – you are driven by thoughts about what you need right now. You identify the essentials and important elements and focus on the present moment.
Transference = Fear

Guilt – not necessarily a negative motivation, this means you have a craving to fix things that are broken and you always want to work out a solution.

Transference = Hope

Innocence – this is a unique Variable and means you have no specific drive. You are powered by true authenticity, which propels you to always do what is right for you.

Transference = Desire

If you have a left-facing arrow, you are designed to get into the nitty-gritty of a situation. Diving deep into all the information available to you will help you better understand it. Never ignore the details.

If you have a right-facing arrow, you need to experience things in a way that suits you, rather than by conventional methods. You have a free-flowing approach to understanding a situation and can spot hidden patterns, taking in the bigger picture of life around you.

BEYOND THIS BOOK

BEYOND THIS BOOK

You may have almost reached the end of this book, but your Human Design journey is only just beginning. Living your Human Design can encourage so much more joy, magic and ease to flow into your life (because it is already within you), although it does require a little consideration at the start. The best way for you to live, to experience the world, is by living in the manner that is most true to your own unique Human Design. And if you are ready to dive deeper, I would suggest reading my recommendations in the Further Reading (see page 227), which offer a more nuanced discussion than there is space for in this book.

So, where shall we start? You will have seen that allowing your Strategy, Authority and Type to lead your life will make the biggest difference to your days, but throughout the preceding chapters you will have also noticed elements that resonate with you more deeply. Remember those passages that made you gasp, laugh out loud or raise your eyebrows in recognition? Perhaps you were nodding along to every word describing your Type? Maybe you are at a pivot point where you are being confronted with big decisions? Have you realized you are living the opposite of your Strategy? The sections that you are already drawn to, which feel most like you and resonate with your current situation, are where you should take your next steps.

KEEP A HUMAN DESIGN DIARY

Commit to journalling your experiments and experiences over the forthcoming month. A full 28-day cycle is necessary for you to travel through all the potential lunar influences. Check in with yourself at the start *and* end of each day to consider the following prompts:

* How do you feel mentally and physically?
* Have you honoured your Type's energy needs?
* Did your Not-Self Theme surface at any time? If so, what were you doing, and where?
* Who are you spending time with?
* Who are you are drawn to?
* What feelings arose around your interactions with each person or group?
* What have you been doing both at work and in your downtime?
* What skills or activities made you excited? And on the flip side, what drained you?
* Can you make space for more of what fires you?
* What decisions did you make?
* How did you connect to your Authority?
* Did you honour your Strategy during the day?
* What made you feel the closest to your Signature?
* Were there ways you ignored your Design? If so, what happened?
* What elements could you change tomorrow to continue your experiments?
* What could you have done differently today?

If there are decisions you regret today (or at any point in the past), remember that you made those choices due to societal conditioning. So, *please* release any guilt. Forgive yourself and move on.

AFFIRMATION: I am not responsible for decisions that are made through the weight of my conditioning.

By looking back at your day, or preparing for the day ahead, you will notice when you are living in accordance with your Strategy and Type, and when you felt aligned. The more aware you are of your Signature and Not-Self Theme, the more you will be able to spot their influence. Living in your Signature is a delicious space to inhabit. Conversely, noticing your Not-Self Theme is not a 'bad' feeling, it is just little nudge from the cosmos to get you back on the right path. As you attune to your Human Design, you will be able to notice any negative self-talk that arises too... and shut it down fast.

Moving from mind-led thinking to each decision being guided by your Authority is a huge ask. Initially your brain will need proof that you are thriving, but by journalling you are collecting evidence that living in this way *does* work. It is also helpful to practise listening to your Inner Authority for even the smallest questions – 'Shall I have a sandwich or salad for lunch?' – so when any big decisions arise, you will be attuned to your inner guidance system and will not miss the prompts. Put your mind into 'observer mode': imagine you are simply watching the movie of your life while your Authority and Strategy make the decisions.

As we are all individuals, everyone on the planet will have a unique approach to living their own Human Design, so try not to get bogged down in being 'correct' or 'perfect'. Starting with baby steps, or even starting over, you will still reach your designed destination. The universe wants you to live as easily as possible, so the less mental, emotional and physical energy you waste, the more aligned you will become.

AFFIRMATION: I allow my unique intuition to guide my decisions.

DECONDITIONING

A crucial step in living your Human Design is deconditioning; removing the conventional thinking you have picked up from a lifetime's exposure to ready-constructed belief systems. Deconditioning takes a seven-year cycle, and even then, you will still slip into 'should' mode from time to time. We are only human! Deconditioning is neither an easy nor a fast fix, but shedding societal expectations and preconceptions will help you start to live authentically aligned to your Human Design. You may bristle at this concept, but be reassured that it is rooted in psychology. As we go through life, we are shaped by outside influences. In psychology, this is recognized as cognitive bias, which can lead to distorted beliefs and thoughts. It is accepted thinking that reducing cognitive bias is helpful in managing anxiety and depression, which echoes the Human Design theory that deconditioning will also release stress and worry, thereby improving our entire lives.

Most conditioning occurs before we reach the age of seven (our lives follow seven-year cycles because that is how long it takes for all our cells to renew), so by now you will have taken in years of (unwanted) opinions from parents, family, friends, teachers, colleagues, media outlets, authorities and governments. These are likely opinions about who you should be and how you should act, and you will have had a value ascribed to your place in the world.

While we need to be around others to understand different points of view, to gather information and to learn, be aware that if you notice you are changing yourself because someone else presents a better way to *be* or they insist that you *should* be doing something they are doing. That is when your conditioning is resurfacing. It will often appear around your undefined Centres, so flick back to Chapter 7 to see if there is an affirmation you can use to remind yourself and allow you to move back into your own Type and Authority.

Instead of being confused by a barrage of outside opinions, listen to your own perfect inner guidance system. Rather than allow your brain to be weighed down by all the options, go with your Inner Authority's wisdom. Move on from anxious feelings and lean into the knowledge that your own body knows the right thing to do. It is hard to give up control of your days by using your mind. Your mind may hold back from those things your Inner Authority yearns for, and vice versa, so you may have to live outside your comfort zone while you acclimatize, but following your Inner Authority is the ultimate way for you to live. Remember that your Authority – and the universe –

wants you to be fulfilled, happy and provided for, so it will always give you a nudge towards the right next step, as long as you are listening.

As you move through the deconditioning process and experiment with your Human Design, you may find things in your life that you need to move on from. Facing your fears is the way to diminish these elements. We are all scared of the unknown and not having the knowledge of what will happen next, but the best method is to acknowledge and respect your fear and then move on. Do not let fear stand in the way of living.

It is terrifying leaving a failed relationship, resigning from a job that is not right for you or speaking out on something you believe in, but these are the practical ways you can remove something outdated in your life to make space for an even better reality. When your mind sees that nothing awful happens (in fact, it is the opposite), it will start to believe in the act of trusting your Authority. If you journal, you will also have stone-cold proof of the improvements in your life, which you can read back to remind your mind.

You may also find that meditation helps your mind to take a back seat. When your mind is quieter, you will be calmer. Who would not want to remove your brain's incessant chatter or replaying of that cringy conversation with your ex/boss/barista at 3am?

AFFIRMATION: I release everything I have been conditioned to accept and allow my true nature to shine.

DEEPER LEARNING

If you have felt the benefits of trusting your Strategy and Authority, moving away from mind-led thinking, you will be eager to explore other ways Human Design can benefit you. We touched on some of the deep-dive elements of the system in Chapter 9 and looked at your personality Profile in Chapter 8. Go back and choose a section to experiment with, then work through each section in turn. Human Design is a system of self-validation that you can explore for the rest of your life, but it is up to *you* to decide which parts are right for you right now. You could spend time investigating both sides of your Profile (your conscious and unconscious traits); find a video that will reveal the nitty-gritty of your Gates and Channels or read a blog post on your Incarnation Cross.

When it comes to your Variables, this is where the real experimentation can begin. Eating when you should or taking in nourishment at the right temperature are all activities that need close attention, but know that however much you are advised to do something (say, eat one food at a time), if your body does not like it and your Authority says 'no', it is not for you. Although if it *did* feel good, do the same tomorrow. Your Variables are the area that needs the utmost accuracy on your birth time, so this is where elements that might not chime can be found. Equally they could provide an 'a-ha' moment that really allows you to live in a way that will nourish and energize your physical body.

AFFIRMATION: I honour my unique Human Design and relax into the perfect flow of life.

JOIN THE COMMUNITY

There is a wonderfully welcoming collective of Human Design followers out in the big wide world, so I would suggest you join an online group for your Type, or stage of learning. Hearing others' experiences is always helpful. Successful practitioners will often build groups of fans on Facebook, Instagram or TikTok, too. When you find a person who offers thinking that rings true with your own recognition of yourself, order a personalized Human Design reading from them. Every book you read or practitioner you follow will have a different interpretation of the basic elements; in the same way you may have a favourite astrologer. The nuances of each reading could lead to deeper understanding of your own Human Design and offer ideas that will help you live more in alignment. In turn, as you gain more knowledge, you could start to share your learnings with your friends and family and provide readings yourself.

AFFIRMATION: As I become inspired, I will also inspire others in my community.

LOVE YOURSELF

Putting yourself first is *not* selfish. This is thinking that we have *all* been conditioned into believing and need to shed, fast. Instead, Human Design asks us to all get reacquainted with our true selves. Fighting against your aura, trying to be someone else or forcing yourself to fit into a box will only cause upset. Instead, living your most authentic life will allow you to be true to yourself. The cosmic bonus is that you will have all the energy required to inspire others and develop a sense of self that others will respect. Consider the people who *you* look up to. Who has the most infectious energy or a sense of self you admire? These are the people who have moved on and ignore judgement, do not seek approval and accept their true nature. You can do this, too, as long as you cultivate true self-love and forgiveness, become confident in who you are and allow your life to simply unfurl.

Some people think that because your Human Design is predestined, it can be restricting, but the knowledge that you can honour your true self is the most freeing state in which to exist! Knowing how you are meant to live will take you to exactly where you should be. Remember that you are perfectly designed the way you are and all your opportunities for greatness, happiness, love and success are already within you. Living life outside the restrictions of the framework of expectation and conditioning will also help you grow a deeper respect for yourself and all you have been through. Appreciate all your magic gifts and unique quirks.

AFFIRMATION: I accept myself exactly as I am.

A NOTE ON 2027

Ahead of us lies 2027, a significant date in Human Design as this is when earth will move into a new cosmic cycle that will impact our entire collective experience. It is not set to be as major as the shift into the Age of Aquarius (see page 5), but it is still a date to be mindful of. Ra Uru Hu shared knowledge of Global Cycles, which follow Eastern and Western astrology and measure the precession of the equinoxes (how long it takes the stars to rotate around the earth's axis, which is about 25,772 years). This planetary activity affects us on earth because whatever happens celestially has the power to influence us energetically, through neutrinos showering the planet (see page 6). Likewise, what happens on earth at this shift will echo the shift in space through societal changes and human evolution.

The year 2027 is when earth will transition from the Cross of Planning to the Cross of Sleeping Phoenix. The Cross of Planning has been the cosmic standard since the seventeenth century and represents tribal groups, foresight and organization across the globe through business and industry. The Cross of Sleeping Phoenix is characterized by rebirth, surrender, transformation and a collapse of conventional boundaries. It is utterly individualistic and this may be played out through a potential breakdown of traditional accepted structures (perhaps heralded by the financial crash of 2008 and then Brexit). We will all move into an age of enlightened selfishness, or individualism, during which we all need to take care of ourselves first.

AND FINALLY

The universe has your back. It always wants you to get the best results and live in a state of ultimate ease and joy where your whole life flows. Human Design gives you the knowledge and actions that will allow you to become the very best version of yourself. Know that your place on this planet is all part of a bigger picture – your role here is *essential* – and being attuned to yourself is not only the best route for *you* to take, but for the future of all those around you. Decoding your individual mission is a lifelong journey of experimentation, tweaking and trying again but deep diving into your Human Design is more rewarding that you can believe. Unlocking your Human Design toolkit is just the beginning.

FURTHER READING

BIBLIOGRAPHY

Shayna Cornelius and Dana Stiles, *Your Human Design* (Fair Winds Press, 2023)
Chetan Parkyn, *Human Design* (HarperCollins, 2009)
Rachel Lieberman, *A Modern Guide to Human Design* (Gibbs Smith, 2023)
Jenna Zoë, *Human Design* (Hay House, 2023)

WEBSITES AND RESOURCES

www.3ho.org
www.ahumandesign.com
www.allure.com
www.almanac.com
www.aquariansigns.com
www.arawme.com
www.barneyandflow.com
www.blackgirlshealinghouse.com
www.bookyogaretreats.com
www.centreofexcellence.com/human-design
www.christieinge.com
www.daylunalife.com
www.elleundefined.com
www.faceyogaexpert.com
www.featherandfoe.ca

www.findyournaturalgroove.com
www.flowwithhumandesign.com
www.geneticmatrix.com
www.goodomen.com
www.headspace.com
www.helloastrology.com
www.human.design
www.humdes.info/generator
www.humandesignblueprint.com
www.humandesigncollective.com
www.humandesignme.com
www.humandesigntools.com
www.innerself.com
www.jessicadavidson.co.uk
www.jovianarchive.com
www.jupiterjewel.com
www.justfollowjoy.com
www.kaiaalline.com
www.kellykubiak.com
www.kmbcoaching.com.au
www.livinglifeinbetween.wordpress.com
www.manifestinghumandesign.com
www.medium.com
www.momonaspiritualjourney.com
www.monrk.co
www.mybodygraph.com
www.myhumandesign.com
www.myhumandesign.com
www.peterberv.com
www.projectormovement.com
www.puregenerators.com

www.projectormovement.com
www.ra.uru.hu
www.reddit.com
www.sanctuarybykristenrice.com
www.soulquartz.com.au
www.theauramarket.com
www.thesimply.ca
www.thewildpixel.com
www.theeverygirl.com/human-design
www.verywellmind.com
www.vogue.in
www.wholeandunleashed.com

ACKNOWLEDGEMENTS

THANK YOU...

To Hayley Southwood for introducing me to Human Design.

To all my friends and family, who I pestered for birth times and locations, and who shared their invaluable feedback on what resonated.

To Stephanie Milner, my literary fairy godmother. If you hadn't spotted me on the street back in 2016 (perhaps even earlier?) and known my obsession with all things hippy and high vibe (as well as my love for shoes and Earl Grey) this book wouldn't be here.

To Lucy Smith and Shamar Gunning – what a pleasure to work with you!

To Lily Wilson – for her excellent design. Laura Russell and the rest of the team at HarperCollins.

To my parents, Christine and Tony. Without your devoted and ongoing provision of unpaid grandparental childcare and chauffeur service, this book would have been a far more convoluted creation, or at least would have been filed way past my deadline. You are the bedrock of our family and we all love you both so very much.

To Colum, you are amazing, wherever and whenever you were born.

INDEX

addiction 48
affirmations 217, 218, 221–2
    and Authority 109, 113, 116, 119, 122, 125, 129, 132
    and Centres 144, 146, 148, 149, 151, 153, 155, 157, 159
    and deconditioning 219, 220
    and Type 53, 61, 69, 77, 84–5, 223
Age of Aquarius 4, 5, 101, 154, 224
Age of Pisces 4, 5, 8
Ajna Centre (Awareness Centre) 141, 144–6
amethyst 61
anxiety 23–4, 101, 114, 141, 142, 143, 159, 218, 219
appetite 204
archetypes 8, 164–85
Aron, Elaine 73
astrology 4–5, 8, 40, 45, 224
Auras (electromagnetic energy fields) 7–8, 10, 37, 39, 45, 197, 223
    closed 62–4, 66–7
    discerning and resistant 78, 80, 83
    extent 39
    focused and penetrating 70
    open and inviting 46–7, 50, 54–5
authentic living 24, 39, 77, 89, 102
Authority 3, 18, 25, 33, 37, 39, 90, 99–132, 139, 189, 191, 196–7, 215, 221
    and Centres 142–4, 146–7, 149, 151, 153, 155, 158
    and decision-making 23–4, 99–132, 101
    and deconditioning 219–20
    Ego-Manifested 120–2
    Ego-Projected 117–19
    Emotional 104–9, 111, 131
    and journalling 217
    Lunar 104, 129–32

    Mental/Environmental 126–9
    and Profile 172, 176–7, 179–80
    Sacral 110–13
    Self-Projected 123–5 and sound healing 27
    Splenic 113–16, 152
    and Strategy 95–7
    and Variables 202

belonging 17
bipolar disorder 108
birth, time of 8, 34–5
birth-time rectification 35
black tourmaline 61, 69
body, messages of 97, 101, 103, 108–13, 128–9
Body Graph 9, 33, 36–9, 41
    and Authority 127, 129
    and Centres 117, 137–8, 146, 151, 198
    and Definition 197, 198
    and Gates 176, 193, 194
    and Incarnation Crosses 190–1 boundary-setting 68, 73–4, 76, 84, 157
brain 19, 23, 36, 38
    brain-led (mind-led) decision-making 46–7, 101, 103, 106, 109, 111, 115, 126, 127, 217, 221
breathwork 26
Buddha 10
burnout 55, 65, 67, 92, 157

calcite 85
carnelian 52
caves 208
cellular regeneration 19
Centres 4, 10, 18, 38–9, 41, 134–59, 189–90, 194
    Defined 138–52, 154, 156–8, 198
    and Definition 197
    and Gates 193
    Open 139
    physical symptoms of misaligned 137–8

    Undefined 138–41, 143–9, 151, 153, 155, 157, 159, 198, 219
    see also specific centres
chakras *see* Hindu Brahmin chakra system
    change, activation 20–1
Channels 38, 39, 138–40, 146, 190, 193–7, 221
    defined 194–5
    undefined 194
chrysocolla 61
citrine 52, 69
coaching 18
codons 9, 41, 193
Cognitive Behavioural Therapy (CBT) 18
    communication skills 92, 146–8
comparison culture 17
conditioning 4, 16–19, 24–5, 139, 217, 219, 223
    and Authority 105, 107, 113, 120
    and Profile 177
    and Type 50, 71, 82–3
    see also deconditioning
    conformity 16
conscious traits 37, 163–4, 167, 194, 221
consciousness 36
creativity 55
crystals 4, 52, 61, 69, 76, 85
cultural appropriation 10–11

dark matter 7
decision-making 17, 96
    affirmation for 218
    analytical 23
    and Authority 23–4, 99–132, 101 and decision fatigue 101
    and gut instinct 23, 46–7, 49, 52, 53, 96
    and intuition 96, 101, 113–16, 123, 127, 129
    and lunar cycles 78–9, 94–5
    mind-led/brain-led 22–3, 46–7, 101, 103, 106,

109, 111, 115, 126, 127, 217, 221
and the subconscious 23
and Type 46-7
deconditioning 24, 39, 46, 72, 105, 218-20
diaries 18-22, 28
Definition 38, 197-200
  Quadruple Split 197, 200
  Single 197, 198
  Split 197
  Triple Split 197, 199-200
  Undefined 197, 198
deoxyribonucleic acid (DNA) 9, 41, 193
depression 108, 141, 142, 159, 218
Design line 163, 167, 190, 194
desire 210, 211
Determination/Digestion (Variable) 38, 204-5
diet 17, 48, 56, 64, 80-1, 190, 204-5, 221
divination methods 4, 9
  see also I Ching

Earth 190, 202
Ego Centre (Heart Centre) 117-18, 120, 141, 150-1
Ego-Manifested Authority 120-2
Ego-Projected Authority 117-19
Emotional Authority 104-9, 111, 131
emotional intelligence 101, 107, 154
emotions 21, 137, 138, 153-5
empathy 74, 78, 92, 107, 119, 127, 140, 155, 168
energy 7, 45, 101-2
  and Centres 137-40, 142, 144-53, 156-9
  exertion 4
  and Generators 46, 49, 51, 53, 91-2
  and Incarnation Crosses 190
  and Manifesting Generators 54-6, 58-9, 91-2
  and Manifestors 62, 64-7
  and Projectors 71, 73-4, 76-7, 117
  and Reflectors 78, 80, 83-4, 95
  and Strategy 91-2, 95
  energy centres see Centres
Environment (Variable) 38, 206-8

equinoxes 5, 224
essential oils 53, 61, 69, 77, 85

Facebook 222
fear 109, 113-14, 210, 220
fluorite 76
fortune telling 8
friendships 168-71, 178, 182

G Centre (Identity Centre) 141, 148-9
G-centre chakra 123-4
Gates 9-10, 38-9, 41, 176, 193-7, 221
  and Centres 139, 140
  defined 193-5
  and gifts 190 how to use 195-7
  and Incarnation Crosses 191 and Reflectors 79
Generators (Type) 46-53
  and affirmations 53
  and Centres 148, 156, 157
  and crystals 52
  and Emotional Authority 104
  and essential oils 53
  famous 51
  and gifts 46-8
  needs of 52
  and relationships 50-1
  and Sacral Authority 110
  and the workplace 48-50
genetics 3-4, 7, 11, 40, 102, 193
gifts 190, 195-6
  Generators 46-8
  Manifesting Generators 54-7
  Manifestors 62-4
  Projectors 70-1
  Reflectors 78-81
global crises 15
Global Cycles 224
grief 22
grounding techniques 113
guilt 211
gut instinct 23, 46-7, 49, 52-3, 55-6, 91, 96, 110-13, 147

habits, unconscious 19
  see also conditioning
Head Centre 141, 142-4
Heart Centre (Ego Centre) 117-18, 120, 141, 150-1
hexagrams 9, 41, 193 Highly Sensitive Person 73
Hindu Brahmin chakra system 4, 10, 55, 58, 113, 123-5, 137

hope 210, 211
Human Design 215-25
  community of 222
  as cultural appropriation 10-11 definition 1-11
  improving your life with 13-28 next-level learning 187-211, 221
  origins 6-11
  science of 9, 19, 40-1
  see also Authority; Centres; Profiles; Strategy; Types
Human Design Charts 2, 24-5, 33-9, 104, 163, 201-2
Human Design Diaries 216-18

I Ching 4, 8, 9, 41, 193
Ibiza 6
identity centre (G Centre) 141, 148-9
imposter syndrome 75, 114, 167, 172
Incarnation Cross 25, 33, 38, 79, 190-3, 221
  Cross of Planning 224
  Cross of Sleeping Phoenix 224
  Juxtaposition Cross (fixed) 176, 193
  Left Angle Cross (interpersonal) 192
  Right Angle Cross (personal) 192
individualism 224
Inner Authority see Authority
  inner guidance 96-7, 139, 147
  see also Authority
  innocence 211
Instagram 222
intention-setting 28
intuition 23, 137, 147, 152, 171
  and crystals 85
  and decision-making 96, 101, 113-16, 123, 127, 129
  and Reflectors 78, 82
Investigator, The (Profile) 164-5, 167-70

Japan 17
journalling 20, 216-18
Jungian psychology 41

Kabbalah 4, 10
kitchens 207
Krakower, Alan (Ra Uru Hu) 6-7, 10-11, 34, 40, 189, 224

labradorite 85
light 205
'living your best life' 24-5, 215, 223
love 164, 168-9, 172-4, 176, 179, 182-3, 185
see also self-love
Lunar Authority 104, 129-32
lunar cycles 78-9

malachite 76
manifestation 75
    Manifesting Generators (Type) 54-61 and affirmations 61
    and Centres 156, 157
    and crystals 61
    and Emotional Authority 104 and essential oils 61
    famous 60
    and gifts 54-7
    needs of 60
    and relationships 58-9
    and Sacral Authority 110 and the workplace 57-8
    Manifestors (Type) 62-9
    and affirmations 69
    and crystals 69
    and Ego-Manifested Authority 120 and Emotional Authority 104
    and essential oils 69
    famous 68
    and gifts 62-4
    needs of 68
    and relationships 66-7
    and Splenic Authority 113 and the workplace 65-6
markets 207-8
me time 20
meditation 26-7, 114-15, 220
    guided 26
Mental/Environmental Authority 126-9
metaphysics 3, 4, 8 mind
    emotional 101
    logical 101, 102
    mind-led (brain-led) decision-making 22-3, 46-7, 101, 103, 106, 109, 111, 115, 126, 127, 217, 221
    releasing your 22-8, 26
mindfulness 22, 97

moonstone 85
Motivation (Variable) 38, 210-11
mountains 207
Myers-Briggs personality assessment 4
mysticism 8

needs 210
neocortex 36
neural pathways 19
neuroscience 101
neutrinos 6-7, 40, 224
New Age beliefs 4, 8, 9, 118
no, learning to say 46, 49, 50-1, 52, 55, 157
    North Nodes of the Moon 202
Not-Self Theme 4, 21, 33, 37, 41, 102-3, 196
    and Authority 117, 124-5
    and Centres 139, 141, 143, 149, 156
    and Generators 46, 92
    and journalling 217
    and Manifesting Generators 54, 59, 92
    and Manifestors 62, 65, 67
    and Profile 170
    and Projectors 70-2, 74, 93, 124-5
    and Reflectors 78, 81, 83

Observed/Observer dichotomy 206-8
opportunities 191, 196
    and Authority 106, 108, 110, 119, 121-2
    and Profile 179, 182
    and Strategy 89, 90, 91
overthinking 23-4, 101, 115
overwhelm 72, 73, 157

paths 3, 18, 80, 124, 192
personal perspective 209
Personality line 163, 167, 190, 194
personality testing 41
personality type 36, 37, 163-85
    conscious 37, 163-4, 167, 194, 221
    unconscious 163-4, 167, 194
    see also Profile
Perspective (Variable) 38, 208-9
physics 40
possibility 209
power 209

pressure 142-4, 158-9
probability 209
Profile 25, 34, 37, 161-85, 189, 221
    1 The Investigator 164-5, 167-70, 176-7, 179-80
    1/3 The Investigator/ The Martyr 167-70
    1/4 The Investigator/The Opportunist 169-70
    2 The Hermit 165, 169-73, 181-3
    2/4 The Hermit/The Opportunist 170-2
    2/5 The Hermit/The Heretic 172-3
    3 The Martyr 165, 167-70, 173-4, 175-6, 184-5
    3/5 The Martyr/The Heretic 173-4
    3/6 The Martyr/The Role Model 175-6 4 The Opportunist 166, 169-72, 176-9
    4/1 The Opportunist/The Investigator 176-7
    4/6 The Opportunist/ The Role Model 178-9
    5 The Heretic 166, 172-4, 179-82
    5/1 The Heretic/The Investigator 179-80
    5/2 The Heretic/The Hermit 181-2
    6 The Role Model 167, 175-6, 178-9, 182-5
    6/2 The Role Model/The Hermit 182-3 6/3 The Role Model/The Martyr 184-5
    and Incarnation Crosses 190
    and Reflectors 79
Projectors (Type) 70-7
    and affirmations 77
    and Authority 104, 113, 117, 123-5, 126
    and Centres 148, 157
    and crystals 76
    and essential oils 77
    famous 75
    and gifts 70-1
    and manifestation 75
    needs of 76
    and relationships 74 in the workplace 72-3
psychological profiling 41
purpose, sense of 3, 15, 25, 38
    and conditioning 18 and the G Centre 148-9

and Incarnation Crosses 190-2 and Profile 176-7
and Projectors 72
and Self-Projected Authority 123-5
see also Incarnation Cross

quantum mechanics 40
Quarter of Life Themes 191

Ra Uru Hu (Alan Krakower) 6-7, 10-11, 34, 40, 189, 224
Reflectors (Type) 78-85
and affirmations 84, 85
and Centres 148, 157
and crystals 85
and Definition 198 and essential oils 85
famous 84
and gifts 78-81
and Lunar Authority 129, 131
needs of 84-5
and relationships 83-4
and the workplace 82-3
Reiki 4
relationships 17
and Profile 164
and Type 45, 50-1, 58-9, 66-7, 74, 83-4
religion 3, 5, 8, 10
Root Centre 141, 158-9
rose quartz 69
routines, changing 20-1

Sacral Authority 110-13
Sacral Beings 156
Sacral Centre 46, 48, 51-2, 55-6, 59, 71, 110, 114, 141, 147, 156-7
Saturn 19
science, of Human Design 9, 19, 40-1
secularization 8 self
authentic 3, 15, 19, 24-5, 65, 82, 84, 91, 164, 170, 172, 223
best 3
see also Signature
self-acceptance 83
self-doubt 23, 106, 114, 118, 143
self-love 223
Self-Projected Authority 123-5
selfishness, enlightened 118, 121, 224

shadow work 21-2
shores 207
'should' behaviours 19, 24, 72, 139
Signature 3, 37, 41
and Generators 46-7, 49, 51
and journalling 217
and Manifesting Generators 54 and Manifestors 62, 67
and Projectors 70, 72
and Reflectors 78, 80
social media 15
Solar Plexus Centre 104-5, 108, 141, 153-5
sound 205
sound healing 27-8
South Nodes of the Moon 202
'speaking out loud' 63, 93, 113, 121-4
Splenic Authority 113-16, 152
Splenic Centre 113, 141, 152-3
standing out 17
Strategy 4, 18, 37, 39, 86-97, 139, 189, 191, 196-7, 215, 221
and Authority 95-7, 110, 118
and Centres 142, 144-5, 147, 149, 151, 153, 155, 158
and Generators (Wait to Respond) 46, 49, 91-2, 110
and journalling 217
and Manifesting Generators (Wait to Respond) 54, 58-9, 91-2, 110
and Manifestors (To Inform) 62, 63, 65, 67, 92-3
and Profile 172, 176, 179, 180
and Projectors (Wait for the Invitation) 70, 93-4 and Reflectors (Wait a Lunar Cycle) 78, 94-5
and Type 46, 49, 54, 58-9, 62-3, 65, 67, 70, 78, 89-96, 110
and Variables 202
subconscious mind 23
Sun 163, 190, 202
sun signs 4, 37, 45

sunstone 52
supernovae 6
survival 208, 209

Tarot cards 8
taste 204
therapy 18
thirst 204
thoughts, negative 18, 22
thriving 4
Throat Centre 52, 56, 141, 146-8
throat chakra 55, 58, 113, 125
TikTok 4, 222
touch 204
Transference 208-11
Tree of Life 4, 10
turquoise 76
Type 4, 8, 18, 25, 34, 37, 39, 41, 42-85, 90, 97, 189, 215
and Authority 118
and deconditioning 219
and Gates 193
and journalling 217
and working patterns 16
see also Generators; Manifesting Generators; Manifestors; Projectors; Reflectors

unconscious 19, 21-2, 36-7, 163-4, 167, 194, 221
uniqueness, personal 17

valleys 207
Variables 38, 190, 201-11, 221
Determination/Digestion 204-5
Environment 206-8
Motivation 210-11
Perspective 208-9
vernal (Spring) equinox 5
vibrations 27

wanting 209
wave-particle duality 41
Western Astrology 8, 224
work 17
9-to-5 16
and Profile 168-71, 173-4, 177-80, 182-5
and Type 45, 48-50, 57-8, 65-6, 72-3, 82-3

zodiac 8
Zohar 10